Ma

John Alexis Macdonald

VANTAGE PRESS
New York

To all children who have
suffered child abuse

FIRST EDITION

All rights reserved, including the right of
reproduction in whole or in part in any form.

Copyright © 1997 by John Alexis Macdonald
Published by Vantage Press, Inc.
516 West 34th Street, New York, New York 10001

Manufactured in the United States of America
ISBN: 0-533-12139-6

Library of Congress Catalog Card No.: 96-90672

0 9 8 7 6 5 4 3 2 1

From where do you come, my son,
and to where do you curiously journey?
From the spume of a wave flung from the sea
ascending to the crest of life
and then
dispersed in spindrift become at one with Me.

Foreword

In my work as a psychotherapist, I am often asked if there seems to be more child abuse happening now than at other times. I usually answer that we have little information because it is only relatively recently that we have even named and acknowledged child abuse, let alone kept statistical data.

Macdonald's Farm by John Macdonald is an opportunity to hear the words of an abused child of an earlier period of our time in history. The words are all the more moving because this record of harshness, hunger, neglect, fear, and love is presented almost matter-of-factly. Mr. Macdonald needs no additional drama beyond the stark story of his life to show us his isolation and despair.

I believe that many of us want to find a way to heal the pain of our childhood experiences. Adults abused as children often have difficulty believing in their own stories. The process of writing one's own story can bring about an acceptance of the truth. Perhaps the sight of word on paper helps to substantiate reality.

I sincerely hope that Mr. Macdonald's book will inspire others to write their life stories. Most of us have parts of our personal history that we would like to understand and heal; writing can be a method for bringing that about.

I hope that in writing this autobiography, Mr. Macdonald has gained some healing and peace. I want to thank him for sharing of himself so bravely and honestly;

it is an honor to be invited into someone's life in this way.

On another level, this book is a story of a time different in many ways from our own. It was fascinating to learn how the everyday events and needs of people were dealt with in the 1920's and 1930's. The ingenuity of the Macdonald family was formidable, as was their tenacity. So often history is written about the large occurrences, and not the commonplace. This book is also an historical account and can be read from that perspective.

—Bonita D. Zisla, M.A., M.F.C.C.

> All suffering is bearable
> if it is seen as part of a story.
> —Isak Dinesen

1

Why do I write an autobiography? It is became I am impressed by the value of a common uniqueness within every individual. To be sure there is no uniqueness in uniqueness itself, and by that I mean that all people are endowed with the common quality of difference from all others, in which their lives have both changed the world to some degree and been changed by it as the roots of a tree reach down into the soil, wrap about, and conform to the impediments, and thereby develop a different system than ever existed before.

I shall write somewhat differently from the usual autobiographical format. I shall write as if I were another person, viewing this life of mine.

Why? Because I believe writing about John somewhat distances the author from his alter ego to produce a less constrained and perhaps more analytical script.

When does life begin? Is it with the germinal joining of male and female cells, or did it predate biological conception? Was not the beginning of John's life, as well as the beginning of everyone's life, hidden within the elements back through all time of antiquity? Perhaps the word (beginning), as it relates to life, is a meaningless word. John's life, in potential form, must have always existed, a prescient waiting to be quickened. But I must begin somewhere, so I shall start with John's paternal grandfather whose name was not Macdonald but Shumway.

The Shumways were an English, or perhaps Scottish titled family. John's only knowledge of his paternal grandfather, Lord James Shumway, was passed on to him by his father, Daniel, who took the name Macdonald from his stepfather, William Macdonald.

In the annals of British history, Lord James Shumway did not have an uncommon experience when he had an illicit romance with a kitchen scullery maid and sired a child. Berated by the family for disgracing them, he married the young lady, named Serima, and was banished to Ontario, Canada, without means of support.

In Brockville, Ontario, he found work as a dyer of fabrics. In due time a girl child was born and she was followed by a baby boy in 1879. Birthing was difficult and Mrs. Shumway, as quite often happened in those times, died in childbirth of unknown complications. James Shumway undoubtedly fell into a depression and may have taken his own life. His body was found in a nearby lake, and near it was a drifting dory boat with his hat in it.

A young childless Scottish-Canadian couple adopted the boy, and the girl was placed in an orphanage. The boy's name was Daniel, and his stepfather was William Macdonald, spelled as one word without a capital D. What the girl's name was or what became of her is unknown.

Bill Macdonald was a scale mechanic, involved in repairing weighing machines, as they were called at that time. He worked with another Irish-Canadian named James Campbell, and the friendship of these two men was to later have ramifications in the family history.

William Macdonald became disenchanted with business opportunities in Canada and chose to move across the border to the United States, and he became an American citizen. Macdonald first made a home for his English wife and their stepchild, Dan, in Detroit, Michigan, and then later moved to Cleveland, Ohio.

Acting upon Macdonald's recommendation, young Campbell and his newly wedded wife Jean joined Bill Macdonald, and they set up shop together to make and repair scales. The Campbells birthed two sons, Roy and Earl, and a daughter named Ruby, and the children also had a half-brother, Fred. Ruby became Dan's childhood playmate.

Scottish history chronicles a terrible battle of the clans between the Macdonald Highlanders and the Campbell Lowlanders, in which the Macdonalds were massacred en masse in 1692 under the orders of William of Orange. Perhaps faint echoes of their jousting may have drifted down through the centuries to this joint venture, the scale business, because the relationship between Macdonald and Campbell was soon faulted and the partnership broke up. William Macdonald began working for a large scale company, which equipped him with a private rail car filled with tools of the trade, and in which he toured the Midwest states repairing wagon scales and industrial scales. As time went on, the business trips became of ever longer duration till finally all home ties were broken and Bill Macdonald never returned to his wife and stepchild. Dan, a skinny lad, was just seven years old when he and his stepmother were left to fend for themselves as best they could.

Dan recalled selling Cleveland newspapers to the business tycoon John D. Rockefeller, Sr. The paper sold for three cents, and Rockefeller often sought Dan out, because he was such a sickly emaciated child, sympathetically awarding Dan a whole nickel for the paper.

Reduced to sudden poverty, Dan's mother survived the crisis by turning her home into a boarding house for nurses. It was a providential decision for when Dan became ill with typhoid fever, the nurses found a hospital bed for him in the sailors and soldiers hospital; an incongruous arrangement in which Dan, age eight, and in the third grade of grammar school was bedded in a ward occupied by men recovering from severe alcoholism. He became witness to patients suffering the delusions of delirium tremors.

Dan's recovery was slow and uncertain. He remained in the hospital for thirteen weeks, and when he did leave he was too debilitated to reenter school, so that became the limit of his formal education. Some time after his recovery from typhoid fever Dan obtained his first job for which he was perfectly adapted. Skinny and emaciated as he was, he was hired to crawl inside of extremely narrow industrial smoke stacks, when they were being manufactured, to hold a heavy peening tool against red hot rivets while the riveter on the outside hammered the rivet tight to secure the seams of the stacks. He worked twelve hour days along with other children of the same age who would often become so exhausted that they would fall asleep inside of the smoke stack, at which the irritated workman on the outside would bang away with his hammer to awaken the child and demand that he keep on working.

From this intense practical experience, Dan learned that children like him were there to be used by society for the utilitarian business of making a living for their employers, with little or no difference between the tools and gears of industry and the working hands of a child. It was a practical lesson that was so well impressed upon him, that he in turn, would throughout his later adult life use his own children in the same way, utilitarian for "his" ambitions just as he was exploited in his childhood.

Dan and his stepmother, in need of work that was more independent and suited to their needs, developed a small dairy farm on Euclid Avenue. The dairy required a horse, and owning a horse at that time was much like owning a car is today. With great pride they purchased from a trader his first horse to pull his dairy cart. Fred, the horse, was a small compact animal with unusual intelligence, and the animal and boy soon had a good working relationship. Dan recalled that Fred quickly learned the entire milk delivery route so well that Dan could grab an armful of bottles off the cart to deliver to each doorstep in a city block, while Fred, knowing what was expected of him, would trot unattended to the next block where Dan would meet the horse and milk cart for the next series of deliveries in a highly efficient operation.

Dan's delivery route took him past a number of saloons where he would usually stop in for a thirst-quenching stein of beer while Fred was left to doze at the hitching post. Coming out of the saloon one day, Dan was astounded to find Fred was down in a sitting position like a dog setting on its haunches. The men in the saloon all turned out to observe this strange behavior. The bartender said, "Your horse is sick."

Someone suggested that some horses can be taught to sit even though their anatomy is not easily adaptable to this unusual position. It suddenly occurred to Dan that the horse trader had told him that Fred had come from among the animals in a defunct circus, so this behavior was probably a learned trick. Everyone was greatly amused and it was suggested that Fred should be given a bucket of the slop beer that is sopped up from bar spills. Maybe it would urge Fred to get back up on his feet and act in a sober and proper manner. Sure enough Fred nuzzled and snorted in the beer, drank it with apparent relish, and heaved himself back onto his feet, and Dan got back to his milk route. But the event was not to end there, for Fred remembered the attention he got sitting down, and every time thereafter that Dan stopped at the saloon, Fred sat down and refused to get up till he got his bucket of beer.

By this time Dan was already a beginning alcoholic, and he related that often when he left the last saloon on his route, having imbibed generously, he would fall asleep while driving the dairy cart. But Fred knew what was expected of him and would saunter along homeward down the middle of Euclid Avenue along the street car tracks with Dan sound asleep. The street cars would come up behind the dairy cart with the motorman tinkling his bell to urge Dan to move over so the street car could pass. With Dan asleep and the horse left to his own free will, Fred was totally indifferent to the needs of the street car and would just nonchalantly amble along, paying no attention to the motorman's frustrations, but getting the driver home to the barn all in good order.

Dairying is an extremely confining job, seven days a week with no holidays, for the cows must be milked daily. After a few years, Dan grew tired of the regimen, sold the dairy, and went to work for the Bell Telephone Company, winding phone induction coils. It was an episode of interest only because he told of winding the coils out of pure platinum wire. Metallurgical science had not yet found any great industrial use for platinum, and it was a good electrical conductor and was readily available to this new industry. Dan told of frequent problems from snarling the winding bobbins, and freeing it up by stripping off a few yards of platinum wire (that today would be worth a small fortune), and discarding it when the boss wasn't looking.

The Spanish-American War was on and Dan was now nineteen—just the right age for the military. He and some of his friends, in a patriotic gesture, applied for enlistment in the army. The enlistment physician looked over Dan's puny body and said, "Get out of here, kid. You're just too skinny." It was fortunate for him that cannon fodder requires robust bodies.

Again Dan's propensity for entrepreneurship led him into renting an onion farm near Cleveland, Ohio. He hired strong Polish peasant women to do the hard work of hoeing and weeding. Dan was astonished by the tough vitality of these women farm workers. They would take one day off to deliver a baby and be back in the field hoeing weeds the following day. The infant was placed in a basket under a tree, and was nursed in the field as was needed. They garnished their black bread lunches with onions, which they ate like apples. Life was harsh and demanding.

During these various business adventures, it is not clear what became of Dan's English stepmother. He spoke of her fondly, but he may have abandoned her just as his stepfather had abandoned him, for about this time Dan moved to Detroit, perhaps responding to the newspaper ads of a man by the name of Henry Ford, who was hiring workers to build a new kind of vehicle driven by gasoline engines.

It was a whole new process called assembly-line production, and it fascinated Dan, but he didn't care much for Henry's peppery nature.

In Detroit Dan seems to have become reacquainted with his childhood playmate, Ruby Campbell, and with her brothers, Earl and Russel. After a romantic interlude, Dan and Ruby were married and soon started a new family. Dan's father- and mother-in-law, the Campbells, only reluctantly endorsed the marriage. Dan and Ruby's first child was Helen Dorthy, born September 26, 1907. Helen was followed by David Ernest, May 12, 1910.

Dan by this time had acquired a combined grocery store and meat market, and the business prospered. Dan told of making sausages using meat amply spiked with stale bread soaked in water to give it weight, which perhaps partly explains the high profits. When Helen was five years old, she recalled in later life, there was a traumatic family experience, the store and house burned to the ground in the middle of the night. The children were hurriedly taken to a neighbor's house where they watched the conflagration in horror. The fire probably left the family penniless, for there was no insurance. Helen vaguely remembered that the family temporarily moved in with the neighbor, and a short time later into a tent.

But Dan picked himself up, and always the optimist, began looking about for a new beginning. Dan's father-in-law, Jim Campbell, who had founded a new scale company in Milwaukee, Wisconsin, had been writing Dan glowing letters of the opportunity there. So Dan packed up the family, moved to Milwaukee, and went to work at Jim Campbell's scale company. As often occurs in similar family enterprises, dissimilar value systems beget irritations, and perhaps Dan's proclivity to alcohol was a problem. There was soon a falling out and angry quarreling. Between Dan and his father-in-law, there was great potential for rivalry in their respective family pride.

The male forebear on the Campbell side of the family was Earl of Farqueston, a man of landed gentry with a large Scottish estate, and a source of pride to the struggling American family. Probably Dan reacted to their pride with a bit of competitive smugness. After all he had his own British ancestry, for which he once held papers, but had destroyed them to exhibit his patriotic spirit in support of American citizenship. Dan was thoroughly American in his views and certainly not inclined to assume prejudicial airs, but in later life, he admitted to a degree of rivalry arising from pedigree. It was inevitable that the family scale business should become merely a brief interlude in the ever growing list of occupations on Dan's job record. It lasted just long enough for Ruby and him to bear another child,

Ronald Russel, born February 1, 1915.

After that event Dan moved again, this time to the remote village of Oconto in northern Wisconsin where he worked for shares on a potato farm. For the children Oconto was a delightful place, but to Dan it was a calamity. The potatoes developed a fatal disease and the entire crop was a total loss. But Helen's memories of Oconto were of long happy walks through the Wisconsin woods with her father as they drove their cows home to be milked. She remembered hearing the terrifying shrieks of panthers and seeing wild wolf packs in the distance stalking the cows. Northern Wisconsin was a remote area in 1915. Helen and David attended school in a one-room school house, with just twelve other children. David was the only child in the first grade. The children's playmates were from German families who spoke no English. But children adapt easily to new languages and Helen and Dave soon learned to communicate as easily with German as they did with English.

After the potato farm tragedy, Dan rented a team of horses and a wagon, packed up the tools and household goods again, and moved the family to a tiny interior Wisconsin village called Stiles. The town name came from the ladderlike steps that were built over the top of the farm fences to accommodate people as they walked across private pastures to get to the village and back.

Helen describes the village as having twelve houses and barns, a store, and a saloon, all painted red. In morning and evening, bawling herds of milk cows were driven through the dusty village on their way to milking barns and pasture.

During the summer Dan took employment in the northern Wisconsin lumbering camps where he remained for the entire season, leaving the family unattended. It must have been hard for Ruby, a young mother of three children, to endure this isolated life in their tiny village.

Before two years had elapsed, Dan's restless spirit overcame him again. He had heard about the need for foundry workers in a little town called Montague in the state of Michigan, near the eastern shore of the Great Lake. World War I was on by that time and the nation's armament industry was tooling up. Dan left Ruby and the children once more and took steamer passage across Lake Michigan to seek a new job opportunity there. It was a lonely time for Ruby and she was harried by worry.

Helen recalled that one day her mother packed a lunch and took the three children on a wonderful train ride to Oconto where they visited a lady, whose name Helen never heard.

Only in later years did she realize it was a very important trip. Ruby and the children returned on the train to Stiles and a week or so passed. Suddenly one day the strange lady, whom they had visited in Oconto, appeared at their house. The children could sense tension and uneasiness in their mother's demeanor. Helen could remember that she and her brothers were sent upstairs to bed early and warned severely not to get back up. Helen did not sleep well, and late in the night she heard moaning and activity. She was terrified by the sounds coming from her mother's room, but she was too well disciplined to leave her bed to find out what was going on. After hours of intermittent sounds and muffled voices, there was a sharp shrieking cry of a baby.

The following morning, February 2, 1917, the strange lady got Helen and her two brothers dressed and took them downstairs to see their mother. There was Ruby propped up in bed, gaunt and tired looking, but happily cheerful too, with a new baby beside her. The children were astonished and David asked, "Where did he come from?" and Helen, with curiosity, asked, "What is his name?"

"I think John would be a nice name," Ruby answered.

Helen was appalled. "John!" she shouted. For unknown reasons Helen associated the name "John" with ugliness and a Neanderthal hairy creature. Some time during her brief life to date she must have seen such a person who was named John and it was imprinted upon her that was what John was like.

Helen thought it was incredible to name a defenseless infant John. But John it was, and the middle name chosen was Alexis, named after a little Russian boy, a childhood friend of Ruby's. Perhaps there was some relevance here in that it was the year of the Russian Bolshevik revolution, 1917.

John was quickened to life during a period of severe tensions, war, insecurity, poverty, family quarrels, restlessness, and endless job-seeking by his father, amid illness and worry on the part of his mother. But it was all part of the pattern of the times that was lived out in the hardships of his forebears struggling to gestate a new order wherein a British lord and a Scottish earl's family would cast aside and abandon their privileged role in the old world to become American citizens in the new world. It was a time of bringing forth sport seeds to begin a new plebian society without the prudish social caste systems and monarchial excesses of Europe. To be sure it was a time of trouble, but it was also a time of great hope.

2

It could not have been long after John's birth that his father came back to Stiles, Wisconsin, to see how the family was getting along, and to announce new plans. Apparently Dan had been away many months because years later he confided to his daughter, Helen, that he had been stunned upon learning that he had a new son. When he left home, he didn't know that Ruby was pregnant. Helen believed that this flight from home was partly in reaction to a family quarrel.

Upon returning home Dan related to his family the following story: From Wisconsin he went to Michigan in 1917, to find work during a time in which he was without funds to support the family and was mentally depressed. He crossed Lake Michigan on a steamer and disembarked in Muskegon, Michigan, from where he had to make his way to Montague, some eighteen miles distant, without money for train fare. So he set out to hike to the village where he hoped to find a job at the Montague Iron Works. En route Dan sat beside the road and an old Jewish rag picker came by in a horse-drawn wagon filled with a variety of salable refuse that he had collected. The Jew stopped to chat and Dan asked for a ride to Montague. The old man welcomed him aboard, and en route Dan aired his problems at some length. The Jew listened attentively to the long story, and the two men spent their time together commiserating on the hardships of life for the whole distance.

When Dan got out of the wagon in Montague, the rag man said, "Wait a minute, young man." He fished around through his load of junk and rags and pulled out an old iron cash box, which he opened with deliberation, took out a ten-dollar bill, and handed it to Dan. Dan was astonished; it was such an unexpected kind gesture. For Dan it completely negated his stereotype of Jews, which he had ingested in the past through many a hurtful prejudicial story, and it became an event that he cherished the rest of his life and never tired of retelling.

When Dan returned from Montague to his family in Stiles, Wisconsin, he was bubbling with enthusiasm about the little town of Montague where he had gotten the promise of a good job at the local foundry there. Montague had a population of about five hundred souls and a very friendly atmosphere. The village had a romantic past in the long-exhausted lumber industry, recounted in the early writings of the author Stewart Edward White.

Dan gathered the family together and packed all their belongings again, and took the train to Milwaukee where they stopped to visit Ruby's parents. Helen remembered the adventure of Grampa Campbell taking her and Dave to the scale factory, near the Lake Michigan waterfront. There he weighed her and Dave on a new wagon scale.

From Milwaukee the family took ship passage across Lake Michigan, with all their household belongings, and made their way to Montague to start a new life. They moved right into a nice rented house on Front Street. It was an exciting new beginning but also an ominous one, for that very night, the house next door caught fire and burned to the ground.

Dan found his new job interesting and remunerative, machining merchant ship propellers on a huge lathe. The privations of the Oconto potato farm and life in Stiles were soon forgotten, and family harmony returned. Ruby now became pregnant with her fifth child. But across the world, times were not so harmonious. World War I was being fought with deepening contortions in a social inferno. Illness, which always follows in the wake of hardship and destruction, was spreading like a black shadow through the ranks of millions of men in the armed services, and moving on across the world in the form of an especially virulent type of influenza. Thousands—perhaps millions—even died. The disease was so common that people shortened the word and merely called it "flu," and flu it has remained in the American lexicon ever since.

Ruby contracted the disease. Helen, who was twelve years old at the time, was terrified and had premonitions of her mother's death, and even planned in her childish mind how she would care for the family.

There is no record of what Ruby's general health was like, but with all the privations of the family and the births of four children, she was probably far weaker than anyone was aware of. Doctors were not readily available then, for many were in the armed services, and those who were left behind to take care of the civilian population were worked beyond their ability to respond. Perhaps Ruby's flu was complicated by pneumonia, and perhaps her pregnancy complicated her illness even further. Dan gave very sketchy accounts of her death. Undoubtedly he did not realize or understand how seriously ill she was. Apparently he was at her bedside when she died at age thirty-eight, and the unborn child died within her. Dan must have been stunned by this swift and irreversible event that probably had never entered his mind as a possibility even.

While Ruby's body was being lowered into a cold grave in the White Lake cemetery, Dan was already making plans to take care of the children. Some men would have deposited them in the nearest orphanage, or farmed them out to relatives. In fact, Grampa Campbell offered to take Helen and raise her, but Dan's bad feelings about his in-laws discouraged that. Dan had a strong will to keep the children together, and Helen was the apple of his eye. To provide for the family, he would have to keep on working at his job, but that would leave the children at home without anyone to look after them.

Dan solved the problem by hiring a widow by the name of Mrs. White to care for the kids. Mary lived in a nice six-room house on Front Street too, and so she took the children there to look after them. It was a sensible arrangement, but this was the first event in an ongoing chain of circumstances that twisted John's character so severely that he really never recovered from it. Mrs. White entered into John's life when he was a two-year-old child, at the time of development when he was forming his first and therefore most impressive and enduring knowledge about humanity.

For Dan to visit the children, he had to frequent Mary White's house. Mary possessed the prevalent Victorian scrupulousness of the times in regard to propitious behavior and appearances. She let Dan know that frequent visitations of an unmarried man at her house during late evening hours, in this small town, was to risk gossip. Neighbors might assume a wrong idea about their relationship. Perhaps a more honest motive for her sensitivity was to bring the situation to Dan's attention to help promote a marriage, for Mary had very little financial means at the time, and Dan must have appeared to her as a lucky find, even considering the obligation to care for his four children. It was difficult for a single woman in a small town, like Montague, to make a living in 1919. Mary's only means of self-support consisted of doing hand laundry, ironing clothes, and sewing for village people.

Mary was not a comely woman. She was about five foot three inches tall, with a squatty, pendulous body, broad squarish face, sharp dark eyes, and graying black hair combed back and twisted into a tight bun at the crown of her head, compressing her short neck. When actively working, coils of fat about her stomach and arms flopped to and fro with her movements. She had a peasantlike profile.

Mary's parents had been poor, uneducated French frontier people, and probably among the first Europeans to colonize the Great Lakes region of Michigan and Wisconsin. Mary had almost no formal education, but she had a sharp animal craftiness and an innate psychological knowledge of how to thrust and parry in the realm of the subjective human psyche. She probably came out of a cruel dysfunctional family and had learned well how to administer psychological as well as physical pain to those in her charge, and to do it in such a way, and at such a time that it would be unobserved by witnesses. But Dan, of course, did not know she had these skills. She must have appeared to him to be an opportune blessing at just the right moment in his and her life. Mary was nine years older than Dan was, but that didn't bother him. Of utmost importance to Dan was the fulfillment of his need for someone to care for and make a home for his children.

Mary and Dan were married quietly in the local Presbyterian church, flanked by Mary's two sisters, Lucy and Maud, and their husbands. The Campbells did not attend. Ruby's death and the somewhat questionable circumstance of her sick care were too recent a happening for them to feel much interest in Dan's hasty marriage. But they probably too thought it would be best for the children. Marriages along strictly utilitarian needs were common at that time. Protestant ethic in the little towns and villages of the Great Lakes region was a vast body of inhibitions and rustic taboos in the early twentieth century. In the minds of some people, marriages springing from the motive of love alone were not grounded in stability.

In view of the limited possibilities open for single women, especially widows, to make their living in 1919, no one could really fault Mary White for making a bid to marry a strong man as her provider, even assuming that it may have been without the incentive of love. And so it was that Dan moved in with Mary at her house on Front Street, and the family was at oneness again. Helen and David were entered into school, and the first memories and impressions of life were stirring in John's age two mind. Dan took this opportunity, of family readjustment, to find another job in his ever-restless odyssey of career management. He went to work in Muskegon, Michigan, at a factory called Continental Motors.

Continental Motors made fine gasoline engines that powered the then popular Durant motor car. It was an exciting time—the terrible war was over and people were optimistic about the future. It was the dawn of mass production of consumer wares. Dan soon rose to become superintendent of the repair division and was very proud of his achievement, and he was probably already dreaming of a future way to develop Mary's farm that he had acquired by his marriage. All the trials and troubles of his first marriage were behind him. The only cloud on his horizon was one that he would never have recognized, alcoholic dependency.

The first memory that stirred and remained in John's mind from early childhood was just a fleeting impression, nothing more, of lying on a bed in his father and stepmother's room and there was a gentle breeze wafting the gauzy lace window curtains. It was neither a pleasant nor an unpleasant impression; it was just an impression of an otherness outside of himself. A second impression, of unknown time later, was coupled with happiness and well-being on a warm summer day. He remembered his sister Helen bundling him into a black baby carriage, and she and another girl wheeling him to the beach at White Lake. It was a very pleasant experience, as can be imagined from the fact that the memory lasted a lifetime.

It emphasizes the importance, in the life of a child, of human interaction during the dawn of an infant's mind. After that there were impressions of the house in both winter and summer, with winter producing the greatest emotional imprint.

The family drew together in the winter. The house was a sheltered island wherein they supported each other against the common enemies, snow, cold, gloom, and mental depression. There was a common defense against the winter in many ways. There were the routine chores of necessity followed by evenings of card games, checkers, dominoes, reading books and magazines, and even darning socks and mending clothes. Each boy darned his own socks, which were usually home-knit. Occasionally the children had sledding parties, which Dan entered into with enthusiasm. There were suppers of hot soup and winter evenings with a warm coal fire in the pot-bellied living room stove. But the defense against winter never seemed to be quite as strong as the cold enemy, for Michigan winters were bitterly cold then. Yet it should not be assumed that this family was like a cozy scene in a Currier and Ives print either. Under the surface of the demands for survival by functional family relations, were deep counter currents of a darker nature invisible to the casual observer.

From the shelter of the clapboard house, John could gain a bleak view of the world outside, oak and maple trees naked of leaves, snowdrifts piled up against the barn and outbuildings, and White Lake with an unbroken frozen surface in the distance. He was looking through small sash windows frosted over at the edges with inverted minaret icicles thrusting down from the roof eaves. Indoors the kitchen was painted with calcimine, a paint made from lime with a colored pigment. The walls were dingy green, darkened further by the sooty smoke of kerosene lamps. At one side of the kitchen was a large varnished bench top cabinet with huge bins that swung out to hold a hundred pounds of flour, and fifty pounds of beans, and perhaps fifty pounds of corn meal, and large quantities of other food staples. These items were fully stocked for the winter against the times when it would be too difficult to go to town during storms and blizzards.

At one side of the kitchen cabinet was the doorway to another little room, the pantry, which had shelves and cupboards in it for dishes, pots, and pans, and where prepared food like bread, meat, and butter was stored. There was no ice box, and refrigerators had not yet come into common usage. The pantry was kept under lock and key to prevent pilfering by the children. On the other side of the kitchen cabinet was another doorway opening onto a landing with a stairway leading down into the cellar.

The cellar was a damp, dark mysterious room beneath the kitchen. The room had an earthen floor and was lined with shelving of rough unpainted lumber on which were stored hundreds of mason jars filled with canned fruits and vegetables that were put up each summer from the family garden and orchards. On the cellar floor were open baskets of potatoes, carrots, and onions, and usually a few hubbard squash. Also there would be a sack or two of dried corn on the cob, which was used as chicken feed. Hanging from the ceiling were smoked hams and bacon encased in muslin flour sacks, and of course there was always a crock of aging beer being prepared for bottling. During winter a barrel of apples was buried in the back yard beneath the frost line and covered with insulating straw, and from which the winter apples were retrieved as needed. All of this, the pantry and cellar foods, and the apple barrel, was off limits for the children who would be severely punished if they got into the food supply. In spite of the ample amount of provisions, the children were kept on scanty rations and were always hungry.

There was a thriving mouse population in the cellar, and from time to time, an ancient black-and-white cat named Teddy was placed down there to stalk "the little beasts," as they were called. But there were so many mice and the years weighed so heavily on Teddy, that very often he would just curl up on a shelf and go to sleep.

Perhaps, in cat language, he was saying to himself, "To hell with it. Why should I knock myself out at my age for a mouse?" According to John's stepmother, whose word was not too good, Teddy was twenty-three years old when he died. It may have been that his long life was in part brought about by an equanimity and easy relationship with mice.

On the opposite side of the kitchen from the cellarway and pantry was a large black cook-stove with baking oven beneath the firebox, and a warming oven above it. The stove chimney passed through the warming oven for utilization of the chimney heat. This was where the homemade bread was set to rise before baking. All the bread consumed by the family was homemade. Fastened to the side of the stove was a water reservoir, heated by the stove, that held perhaps five gallons of water. The reservoir was filled daily by carrying in buckets of water pumped by hand pump from a well in the back yard. The reservoir was the only source of heated water in the house other than a teakettle.

One of the first morning chores each day was to take a small amount of kitchen water (heated in the winter) out to the hand pump and pour it down the throat of the device. In winter this served two purposes at once: it thawed the frozen pump plunger and primed the pump at the same time. The handle was then vigorously stroked up and down till water was brought up from the well and the pail filled.

An amusing game the children often played on freezing mornings was to briefly touch the tongue to the pump handle. If it was left there a second too long, the skin would freeze to the iron surface and pulling it free was a painful experience. It took several buckets of water to fill the stove reservoir and then an extra bucket of water to set aside on the kitchen cabinet to serve as a cold water source for the rest of the day. The bottom of the water bucket was largely covered with lead-soldered holes, so doubtlessly all drinking water was contaminated with lead. A tin dipper, commonly used by everyone to drink out of it, was hung by the water pail. Part of the daily regimen was that each child in the morning was required to drink a quantity of water as a health practice.

Bathing at home was largely confined to winter months because in summer the lake provided for this need. For the children, a bath about every two months was considered adequate. The water for a bath was pumped and then heated on the stove. After heating it was poured into a galvanized laundry tub. Bathing went by age with John, the youngest, going first, and the other two boys afterwards all in the same water, so youth, in this ritual, had the luxurious advantage of clean water. Sister Helen was also provided a fresh tub of water. Ma regarded frequent bathing with skepticism, as self-indulgent nonsense.

Off one side of the kitchen was a tiny room called a bathroom. It contained neither bathing facilities nor a toilet, but there was a small enamel wash bowl on a stand with a cracked mirror over it. It was here that everyone washed and brushed their teeth—that is everyone except John. He was never provided with a toothbrush and never had one through his entire adolescence. Dental hygiene had a very low priority. Decayed teeth were simply allowed to disintegrate. In the so-called bathroom was a primitive slop bucket with a drainpipe soldered into it, with piping that led out to the kitchen garden by which waste water was disposed of. Ma, as John's stepmother was referred to, felt that a real bathroom built inside the house was unsanitary, and anyway it was merely a nonsensical form of self-indulgence, and Dan was indifferent to its functionalism.

There was a privy toilet in a separate little building, about a hundred feet behind the house, containing a bench with two commode openings to accommodate two persons at the same time. The privy walls were papered over with old newspapers to prevent snow from drifting in through the cracks. The toilet paper consisted of a last year's Sears mail-order catalog with the lady's undergarment section discreetly removed to avoid titillation. The toilet was in questionable proximity to the water well.

During the summer, fecal odors from the privy attracted buzzing clouds of flies that circulated between uncovered food and milk in the house and the toilet. The outhouse shared a wall with the chicken house and it was interesting, while engaged there, to listen to the chickens cackling. One learned that a certain staccato call, with a pleasured emphasis, meant that an egg had been dropped in the nest.

Inside the farmhouse, adjacent to the kitchen, was the living room, a general family room in which the Macdonalds all gathered at night after supper was over and the chores were all done. Here Dan had a handsome leather rocking chair where he read the daily paper, the *Muskegon Chronicle*, and the *Saturday Evening Post* magazine. The children each had their own chair assigned to them in the living room, and it was the rule that no one ever sat in anyone's chair other than his or her own. The focal point of the room was a large beautiful buffet with a mirrored display surface, and prominently displayed on it was an ornate silver tea set that was never used. The room was heated with a pot-bellied stove that had a nickel fender that encircled the base to prevent clothing from contacting the hot surface. The pine wood floor was covered with a threadbare wine-colored rug with a dimly faded design. The walls of the room were papered over with a dismally faded flower-pattern wallpaper that was blotched with stains.

The only other furniture in the living room was Dan's homemade smoking stand and a pedal-driven sewing machine.

Off one side of the sitting room was another room called the parlor, and it was more or less off limits to the children. It contained such items as a foot-pumped ancient organ of ornate design, a spring wound phonograph with records of John McCormack, Enrico Caruso, and other voices popular at the time. There was also an upholstered platform rocking chair, which was buoyed under the rockers with coil springs to produce a more vigorous action. When Dan and Mary were absent, the children secretly and daringly entered the parlor, pumped out wailing notes on the organ, and wound up the phonograph. It was only on those rare occasions such as Christmas that the room was ever used other than as a kind of display room for the best furniture that was considered too good to be used every day. During Christmas season, the room was decorated with a tree cut from the nearby woods, and hung with strings of popcorn, and ornaments.

There were three bedrooms in the house and John and his two brothers occupied one that had a nice window that looked out upon an enormous old oak tree, and beyond that to lovely White Lake, perhaps a mile distant. The wallpaper in this room was what impressed John the most.

It had a dung-colored pattern splattered with innumerable blotches of darker color that indicated where bedbugs had been squashed on the wall. Braided rugs made of old worn-out stockings covered the pine floor. The bedding itself was home-sewn patchwork quilts made from cut-out squares of discarded clothing.

On one side of the room was a crude shelving cabinet covered with a drape. In that cabinet were the crown jewels of the children, a number of toys that had been given to them by their grandparents, the Campbells. Only on very rare occasions did Ma allow the children to play with them, and only at those times when the children took courage to make a special request to their father. The toys could be seen daily but could not be touched for fear of severe reprisal from Mary. For John, the most impressive item was a set of wooden construction blocks that could be assembled variously to form all sorts of model buildings and cars by fitting the pieces together with wooden dowels. Mary was jealous of John's mother's side of the family, and it was from them, the Campbells, that the toys had been given to the children. Eventually Mary burned the set of blocks cruelly to prevent the children from enjoying them. Helen found bits of the burned blocks in the kitchen stove.

Behind the clapboard house was a dilapidated unpainted barn with a tool shed, cattle stalls, garage or carriage area, and a loft. The garage was occupied by a homemade tractor that Dan had built by reconstructing an old motor truck. In one cattle stall was a little Guernsey milk cow with crumpled horns. She gave delicious rich milk.

Near the barn was a pig pen and dung heap. Between the barn and house was a smoke house for preserving hams, bacon, and lake fish. About a mile from the house were the twenty acres of farmland with apple, cherry, and pear orchards, a tangle of concord grapes, vegetable fields, and a cow pasture with a stream running through it.

This was Macdonald's Farm. It was probably a typical small Midwest farm of the early twentieth century. What was remarkable about it, considering its small size, was the degree of self-sufficiency that it afforded the family: vegetables and flowers from the garden, fruit from the orchards, dairy products from the cow, meat from the hogs, eggs and chickens from the poultry pen, fish from the lake, and money from the sale of excess products, and all the family members worked with scheduled precision to make it function like a well-lubricated machine. The key factor was nuclear family discipline that was quite often overbearingly severe.

But the children's lifestyle was not altogether unrelieved dower work. Down a little hill from the house was a play area they named "the swings." Dan had erected two children's swings there suspended from the oak boughs, and there it was that the children, with vast imagination and inventive skill, had built little toy houses, cars, and roads, all out of sticks and stones, with tiny dolls sewn by sister Helen from scraps of rags, and the children breathed life into the toys made by their own hands. One cannot help but compare the rich experience of the children in creating their own toys at that time, with the plastic machine-manufactured products of today. Parents buy all of these sterile mass-produced things from specialized toy stores that leave their children's minds completely unchallenged by inventive imagination. The vast commercial toy industry has robbed modern children spiritually and subjected them to the boredom of surfeit.

Final details of the Macdonald family home and possessions were the boat and boat house Dan acquired. The boat house was in a delightful little cove on White Lake, overgrown with bulrushes and squishy sphagnum moss. John recalled the view down into the scintillating water from inside the boat house with the sun outside illuminating the weedy lake bottom with magic warmth, and minnows darting about through their aquatic garden.

White Lake was a body of water about seven miles long and a mile wide at its widest. It was fed by pristine water from White River. The lake was teeming with pickerel, bass, sun fish, and perch, and populated with muskrats and water birds and innumerable turtles and frogs.

The lake pleasure boats were called launches, and a few were driven by little steam engines, but most of them had primitive gasoline engines. Dan's boat, *The Hilda*, was about fourteen feet long and topped with a gaily fringed canopy. It was driven by a three-cylinder gasoline engine and had a big flywheel that spun and projected out of the side of the engine without any guard. No one was ever even slightly concerned that its rotation could easily catch clothing and cause a disastrous accident. The first ritual for firing up the motor was for Dan to place four mothballs, made of naphthalene, into the gas tank to dissolve. This was presumed to make the engine easier to start and boost its power. The greatest family ecstasy was a Sunday boat ride.

3

John's childhood impression of his stepmother was one of such terror that he would cower like a beaten animal when he was alone with her. Like many boys, he and his brother were bed-wetters. Ma (Mary) had her own remedy for this: she would grab their legs, turn them upside-down, and thrust their heads in a bucket of water. Crying, gagging, and choking, they would be pulled out for a moment of recovery and then repeatedly thrust in again. The fear of this cruel semi-drowning treatment was so traumatic that John learned to control himself for a full day before peeing. When he entered grammar school, the teachers pointed him out to the other children, who were constantly running to the privy, as such an excellent example of self-control. Had they known the terrifying cost of this exemplary behavior, they would have been aghast.

John's stepmother was not only a malicious and cruel person, but she was carefully secretive about it, indicating that she had knowledge of the full culpability for her actions. She probably secretly hated the children. Unfortunately she had John, the youngest child, isolated in the house with her much of the time while Dan was away and the other children were either in school or working on the farm. During these times John lived in constant dread and fear of her anger and tried to make himself as little noticed as possible by cowering and remaining perfectly silent.

Often without provocation she would brutally lash out

with sudden blows, usually to the face and ears, but being very careful not to leave any noticeable injury by striking with the flat of the hand. On one occasion, when John was about four years old, he was sitting on the platform rocking chair in the living room. He was silent as usual because he was afraid to speak or do anything to draw attention to himself when he was alone with his stepmother, but he was amusing himself by rocking gently in the chair. Ma ordered him to sit still.

For a small child to sit quietly without movement for long periods is very difficult. Surreptitiously he began rocking again when he thought she was not looking. Ma caught sight of his movement, approached him livid with anger, and hit him so hard that he turned over backwards in the chair and a deep gash was opened under his left eye bleeding profusely. Mary saw what she had done and became concerned about her culpability. She hastily set to work to staunch the flow of blood. About that time John's father came home for lunch and saw the injury. Mary lied and said the boy had done this to himself, but Dan knew intuitively that it had been caused by her violence and he questioned John about it. But questioning John was fruitless, for the boy knew that if he told what really happened he would set himself up for severe reprisal the next time he was alone with his stepmother.

Dan angrily denounced Mary and a bitter argument followed in which she became very docile and fawning. The episode was closed. Family life went on, but when the wound healed, it left two lifetime scars, one under John's left eye and an even more aggrieved one in his mind.

Undoubtedly Mary felt a secret resentment at being saddled with the drudgery of caring for four children in her marriage of convenience. It meant she had to sustain the drudgery of washing, ironing, cooking, and keeping house for the children, as well as her husband, all of which was done by primitive means. There were no washing machines, no vacuum cleaners, no electric irons; clothes were almost all made by hand, there was no piped-in water, no flush toilet, no electric lights, no refrigerators or appliances of any kind, no gas or electric stove, no central heating. The work of maintaining a family was oppressive and unending from daylight to dark. Perhaps Mary's resentment of the workload the children caused was understandable, but it did not vindicate her cruelty.

Mary's vindictive meanness often came out in sly, obtuse ways that were difficult for outsiders to observe. One of her favorite methods of causing pain was to cause embarrassment for the children.

She would daily force John to sit in the outdoor privy, facing a public street, with the door open to public scrutiny. It was an embarrassing and inhibiting experience. On a number of occasions, she forced him to remove all of his clothes and go outside to the children's play area, in full public view, to pick up scattered toys; and the so-called toys were homemade wooden toy buildings he had made, created from lumber scraps, so to pick them up was to destroy them.

Mary was diabolically clever at devising means of producing pain without physical evidence. One method was the exercise discipline. The family house had a long front porch that reached almost the full length of the house. Whenever no one was home to observe it, Mary would order John to march for hours back and forth, the length of the porch, ostensibly for exercise. To refuse to obey her demands was too frightening to contemplate, so he docilely conformed with a feeling of powerlessness and anger when he could look out at the houses of neighbors where children were playing and enjoying themselves while he was locked in this senseless regimen. Unfortunately for Mary, one day her sister's husband happened by for a visit and witnessed the event. Seeing the obvious meanness of the act, he accosted Mary and angrily denounced her so severely that she never did that again, but that particular form of cruelty was just replaced with other forms with greater subtlety.

One of the most hurtful stratagems Ma used against John concerned reading. John's father acquired a job away from home in Jackson, Michigan, which lasted for many months. During this time Dan wrote letters home to keep in touch with the family and tell them what he was doing. John had a special feeling for his father, who by contrast with his stepmother, was normally gentle with his children although he was a taskmaster and demanded obedience from them. Dan enjoyed many playful times with the children and John adored these special events. Perhaps John's stepmother possessed an irrational envy of this paternal affection and wanted to break up the relationship between father and children.

John was about in first grade of grammar school and just starting to learn to read, and at that time handwriting was beyond his ability to decipher. Now each time a letter arrived from John's father, Mary would give it to John and order him to read it aloud to demonstrate what he was learning in school. This of course was far beyond his ability and she knew that, and besides, Dan did not write very legibly and was an abysmal speller, so there was no possibility of John's reading it. She would then punish him for his stupidity by slapping his face and ears. Aside from the pain of the experience, it created a sense of guilt over not being able to respond to his father, whom he loved. This kind of attempted poisoning of the paternal relationship was also extended, in one way or another, to all the children.

The psychological effect on children, of parental hostility, can be devastating to their human relationships ever afterward. In John, isolated as he was from social contact with anyone other than his stepmother much of the time, it produced the gut feeling, that in general, all people could be expected to be hostile and were to be feared, and he transferred this overwhelmingly negative experience with his stepmother, to a prototype of all humanity. He made a general emotional assessment that all humanity, except his brothers and sister, were dangerous and cruel, leading him to shrink from contact with people, and into an excessive shyness. Although much more defiant and assertive, brother Ron too became estranged by the stress of this relationship and ran away from home for a while in his teen years.

It is now known that dysfunctional family experiences can be passed on from generation to generation till there is intervention and the cycle is broken. John's stepmother probably had the prerequisite twisted childhood of authoritarianism, too, which evoked hostility in her and which she took out on the children. She was forever making ridiculous authoritarian threats, such as telling John that she was going to call the police and have him put into a reform school, or she would call his father to have him whipped, or that she would tell his teachers that they should punish him for being stupid.

For John, rational knowledge had little power over those deep grooves plowed into the psyche of his childhood mind. As the twig is bent, so grows the tree.

John's preschool childhood was a lonely time. His father was busy now working on the farm, and the other children were either in school or working on the farm, too. Everyone left early in the morning and did not return till late evenings. During this time John was stuck with the harsh surveillance of his stepmother. His playground was a grove of oak and chokecherry trees near the house that the children called the swings. John remembered seemingly endless days spent alone at the swings, prohibited from leaving the area or even to go back into the house, and always envious of the neighborhood kids shouting and playing only about a village block away.

Quite often he was left at the swings for whole days at a time in complete solitude. Such was the case in a never-to-be-forgotten episode in which Dan, who loved movies, picked up the other children and Mary and drove them to Muskegon, some eighteen miles distance, to attend the premier showing of the first so-called "talking picture," Al Jolson in *Sunny Boy*. For John, at the swing, it seemed like an endless eternity. He was actually locked out of his own house.

He cried with loneliness till someone—probably a neighbor—saw him sobbing. John remembers the man asking him why he was crying, why was he there alone, and where were his parents? He was too afraid to answer, afraid of the stranger, afraid that somehow he had done something wrong again, and especially afraid of reprisal by his stepmother. During the remainder of the day, he found a dead robin. He cuddled the bird for hours for comfort and afterwards hid the dead bird, and on following days took it out and cuddled it again till it disintegrated. In the meantime the man who had spoken to him, apparently accosted his parents about the episode, causing some acute embarrassment for which John was then verbally punished.

John was subjected to the greatest amount of his stepmother's influence and consequently suffered the greatest psychological injury. But each of the children, in his or her own way, was subjected to the same largely unwitnessed surreptitious ugly abuse by Mary. Undoubtedly each child's life character was altered and shaped by it. Child abuse is healed by distance of years, but the healing always leaves its scars.

At its best, for children on small farms, life is hard highly regimented work that often intrudes on their education. Kids are yanked out of school to help with a harvest or to do the plowing when the soil has the right moisture, etc.

The nursery rhyme song of MacDonald's farm left out a vital piece of information: it doesn't mention farm children. Even though farm life is rich in experiences close to nature, perhaps there has never been a more exploited group of humans than the children on the small farms of early America. The father of the family was the imperial head of the family, not cruel, but as authoritarian as a ship's captain. He had to be in order to make the farm functional. Every member had to work in lock-step before the farm could generate the resources to sustain the family.

Very often one or another of the family could not maintain his or her burden of work because of illness or some other factor and so the farm failed—it failed first in human relations and then failed economically. During World War II, hordes of children who had grown to adulthood on small farms began fleeing to the cities to take up war-related work, and with their farm skills, they became highly valued workers. They rarely ever returned to the confining and regimented farm life.

4

Dan Macdonald's entire career life consisted of a long series of entrepreneurial adventures, starting as a teenaged youngster with a dairy farm, and each new proposition kept increasing in financial magnitude and greater complication. Having acquired a farm through his marriage to his second wife, Mary, he began laying plans to develop the fallow and largely unimproved land into his vision for the family future. He was taken by the idea of growing both flowers and vegetables, and he began by turning part of the quarter acre garden plot at the family home, which was about a mile from the farm acreage, into a truck garden for local marketing. Muskegon, the nearest sizable city, had an open farmer's market at that time, and it was his plan to harvest flowers and vegetables just as early in the spring season as possible, and truck them to the Muskegon market.

It was about this time, 1919, when the village of Montague acquired an electric power grid. Prior to that time, all lighting was lamp light, and all household heating was either wood or coal fueled. Dan, always at the forefront of trying out new technology, wired the family home for electric power himself, and while in the process of doing this, conceived the idea of electrically heated hot bed soil to force early growth of vegetables even before the spring frost was out of the otherwise cold soil.

The more that Dan thought about it, the more he became excited about his idea, for this was a time when transportation was yet too limited and far too expensive to ship produce from such exotic places as California or Florida. Electrical engineering was a relatively new technology then with which Dan did not concern himself too much. The niceties of the requisite values of ohms, amperes, and volts, and the size of the wires could all be learned easily in the process of doing the job.

Dan set to work enthusiastically, assembling a series of glass sash-covered hot beds filled with fertile soil in which he buried electrical heating cables, and with great expectation turned on the power. The house lights dimmed down and a fuse burned out. Replacing the fuse with one of a larger electrical value, he found it too burned out. He was not a man to be discouraged by minor miscalculations—if power requirements were larger than had been anticipated, you simply acquired more power for the job—so he wired around the power meter and fuse box, and took the power directly off of the high voltage bus bars. With the power turned on now, the heating cables did a fine job and lettuce and radishes throve in the warmed soil. He didn't regard intercepting the metered power as a theft. To Dan it was like drawing water from a well; it was there, so why not use it? But now when he turned the power on, not only did his lights dim down, but all the lights in the neighborhood also dimmed down.

Eventually the neighborhood power transformer blew out, causing an area-wide power failure. But in the meantime Dan's vegetables had been basking in the warm soil, and under solar glass panels were growing profusely while the seasonal frost was not yet out of the early cold earth. The power company crew replaced the transformer and just assumed that transformers fail from time to time. For Dan, his plan was a great success. But then a second transformer blew out. At that point in time, Dan had to admit that perhaps his idea for growing early spring vegetables had to be weighed against the down side of blown transformers. For the power company, two transformers failing in the same neighborhood, within such a short time, left their electricians puzzled as to the cause of this mystery.

The warmed soil plan was abandoned, but now long-term ideas were gestating in Dan's mind: Much of the farm was covered with scrub oak and hemlock trees, and dotted with very large old pine stumps—remains from the forest trees that had been timbered off years ago. Brother Dave was about twelve years old then. Dan took him out of school, and with the boy's help, began clearing the farm, cutting down the scrub growth and blasting out the old stumps with dynamite. Dave was taught to drive the tractor and pull the loosened stumps out. They then leveled and cultivated the land, and planted apple trees. In this operation, blasting with dynamite had a great appeal for Dan, perhaps satisfying a masculine urge for violence.

After a few episodes of rocks and stump parts whizzing past his head like cannonballs, Dan became quite skilled at placing dynamite charges and ducking for cover. The explosive could readily be purchased, at that time, without any permit or certification of the user's ability and knowledge of handling. One simply learned from the lethal experience of using the stuff. While Dan was clearing the land, he gained quite a reputation around town for his blasting ability. Consequently a wealthy yachtsman contracted with him to blast out a landing slip for his very large yacht at a place called Mich-ill-inda on the shore of White Lake, so Dan temporarily abandoned the farm. But Dave, at age twelve, was directed to continue the work, blasting out stumps with dynamite, clearing land with the tractor, doing the daily milking, and carrying on all the work of a farm hand during his summer school vacation.

Dan hired a diver to show him how to set the underwater charges in this new project. Always ready to take on new challenges, he couldn't wait to get into the water himself. Without being able to swim even, he donned a diving suit and with minimum instructions and no knowledge about underwater diving, he enthusiastically set about placing his own dynamite charges and proceeded to blast out a trench of sufficient length, width, and depth to float the yacht, then went on to build an accompanying pier to complete the job.

About the time that John reached the second grade in grammar school, something occurred in the family that changed his life dramatically. He was suddenly allowed to socialize with other children in the neighborhood. Prior to this he and his brother Ron were always kept to the confinement in their own yard or the farm except during school sessions, although Ron, being more rebellious, had long taken to venturing away in spite of the restrictions. Perhaps John's father raised objections to Mary's jaillike confinement of the two younger children.

The Phillips house was close by, with a passel of six children in it. One of them was named LaVerne, a boy, who was in John's class in school. Mrs. Phillips was an Irish-American widow with almost no means of support in an endless cycle of poverty. Yet she did what can only be regarded as a heroic job of maintaining the family by staying at home to care for the children, selling homemade bread, doing washing and ironing for townspeople, and whatever other odd jobs she could work at in her home. From time to time, a brother who owned a farm would show up with a load of food to supplement her efforts. Mister Phillips had been a fireman and had died from a heart attack, so perhaps she had a small stipend pension. Anyway, having six children and no husband at a time when women had few opportunities in the labor market must have been a devastating experience.

The Phillips family life was completely opposite in character from John's family where there was severe discipline, forbidden self-expression, children were to be seen but not heard, and where there was often mental and physical cruelty. The Phillips children had wholly free self-expression, were only mildly disciplined, and had a mother who, in spite of poverty, was loving and kind. Naturally the Phillips family was like a magnetic attraction for both John and Ron, and they became so attached to the free happy environment that they became like members of the family, only leaving to go home at night. All the other neighborhood children gathered there too, and summer days were filled with sandlot ball games, playing store with discarded tin cans set on cardboard boxes, hide and seek, tag, shouting, and rough-and-tumble activities in which the house and yard were in bedlam. There is no doubt that the throngs of children drove Mrs. Phillips crazy, but she never complained nor intervened in the onslaught. Freedom in the Phillips family was unabridged.

The Phillips children had another attraction aside from freedom: they also had bicycles. To be sure they were old beat-up vehicles with no fenders, with ragged tires, broken drive chains, and no brakes, but to John and Ron, who had never had access to bikes before, they were a major attraction and they both soon learned to ride. Ron was quite good at mechanical repairs, and he soon had the brakes adjusted and the drive chains repaired.

But the tires were an ongoing challenge, for obviously anyone as poor as the Phillips family was could not buy bicycle tires. Ron came upon the idea somewhere of filling the tires with roofing tar. The theory was that the gummy fluid would find its way into the puncture holes and seal them. A quantity of tar was found and the children all stood about and watched with fascination as Ron liquefied the tar by heating it and then painstakingly poured as much as possible through the valve stems into the tire inner tubes. Now LaVerne, John's friend, was perhaps the most intelligent boy in his class scholastically, but he had a kind of clumsy ineptness in the practical management of mechanical things. So the tires having been cleverly repaired with tar, as a sealer, and inflated with air, LaVerne couldn't wait to try out the bike, unfortunately before the tar had cooled enough yet to congeal, so that as the fenderless bike got up speed, centrifugal force spun it out of the holes in the tires in great looping streams, forming a tar line up LaVerne's back, through his hair, and down his front. The children shrieked with laughter. Such were the happy days at the Phillips house.

After John was finally released by Mary from the confines of his own yard and could now have and make friends in the neighborhood, he became acquainted with Harold Becker who lived across the street in a large rambling house overlooking White Lake. Harold was a small German-American boy who was adventurous and full of fun.

John was astonished to find that Mrs. Becker was Harold's stepmother and that she had a very warm and loving relationship with her adopted son. Prior to his acquaintance with Mrs. Becker, John's only knowledge of stepmothers was that of his own, from which he assumed, that as a class group they were all ogres.

Mister Becker was an interesting old Civil War veteran who loved to tell stories to the kids. He had a special room in the garret of the house filled with his Civil War mementos, his rifle and bayonet, his uniforms and his service metals, and his many books. For John and Ron, the most intriguing item was the rifle, which had a barrel bore about a half-inch in diameter. The bullets it fired must have been truly lethal. The neighbor kids invented a game of challenge with the gun, each trying to hold the rifle out from their shoulders in a straight firing position for the longest period of time, without its massive weight causing it to descend. It was the heaviest rifle John ever saw before or after and attested awesomely to the rugged physique of the soldiers of the Civil War.

Mister Becker was a great fisherman and also an inventive man. He had a little fishing dory in which he had made oars that had knuckle joints in them so arranged that one could sit facing the bow of the boat, pull the oars backward, and yet propel the boat forward, a distinctive advantage over the conventional back facing rower.

White Lake was pristine in 1924 and teeming with fish, so Mr. Becker would row out in the lake, pull in a nice catch of pickerel and bass—using unbarbed hooks so they did not injure their mouths, put the fish live in a bucket of water, and back at his boat landing release them live into an underwater cage. In that way, at any time he chose, he could go down to the lake and select a fresh fish for dinner.

John loved to visit the Beckers and bask in the kind gentle relationship they all had with each other, and to note their smoothly organized lifestyle as contrasted to the Phillips bedlam, or the hostility, discipline, and fear in his own household.

Behind the Macdonalds' family home was a neat, well-kept neighbor's home where the Cranes lived with their one child, Grant, who was much older than John. Grant was a very entertaining lad who could remember and tell endless off-color jokes. He was a stand-up comedian before the term had been invented.

One of John's chores, after getting home from school in

the afternoon, was to take a coal scuttle and an ax out to the back yard, and chop kindling wood to start the cooking stove fire with the following morning. The kindling wood was cut from a large pile of pine stumps that Dan had cleared from the farm and piled up in the back yard. It was a miserable job because at age seven he had neither the strength nor the skill to effectively chop up the flint-hard twisted wood.

One day Grant Crane, seeing John struggle to chop the kindling, came over to the wood yard. Grant had joined the Boy Scouts and part of his scouting merit badge program was to do someone a "good turn" each day. Grant was a husky boy of about sixteen years, and taking his scouting pledge seriously, he offered to cut wood for John. Grant started out with his usual introductory joke and John was delighted especially as Grant laid into the tough pine stumps, making the chips fly. Now John's life had been so bereft of kindness that when someone was actually so kind to him, as Grant was, it overcame his emotional stability with the result that he would cry, not from sadness but from joy.

That was of course confusing to Grant who may have thought his joke had been taken wrong, but worse yet, Ma, who happened to see the whole affair through the kitchen window, came storming out of the house in a rage and ran Grant off the property, for Mary's iron rule was that no neighbor's child could ever visit at the Macdonalds' house, probably for fear that they might find out what terrors were going on there. So Grant's kindly intentioned "good deed" became a disaster, and the boy was astonished as to what had happened.

Grant's mother, Mrs. Crane, probably had some insight into the emotional stress that caused John to cry when he was shown kindness. Mrs. Crane would handle it by asking John to pick her a bouquet of wildflowers, which grew profusely everywhere around the area. John knew a treat was in store for him then.

He would gather a bunch of goldenrod, black-eyed Susans, daisies, and lupines—whatever was blooming—for Mrs. Crane, and she in turn would reward him with the most delicious meat sandwiches, when he never got at home, and often a packet of candy or cookies. Invariably John's reaction was to burst into tears of joy. Mrs. Crane understood, mothered, and comforted him.

Kind acts by people toward John during his childhood were to him like coming upon a verdant oasis in the center of an otherwise barren desert of human relations, and they so overwhelmed him that never in his life afterward was he able to control the emotion that sprang from kindness. The psychological consequence of this reaction was a sort of inverted personality that tended to ignore or even avoid and reject kindness because it could not be handled with equanimity. Therefore perhaps many people in his life regarded him as somewhat socially cold and remote, when in fact he was avoiding social intercourse in an effort to avoid an emotional investment that would get out of control.

In addition to this, he had been so emphatically made to believe that he was stupid and therefore inferior that he never felt adequate enough to become a social person. Knowing and understanding his own infirmities produced a rather tensioned social life, wanting to be social and outgoing, but torn by feelings of low self-esteem, and always fearful of the lack of emotional control in the event that people were kind to him.

In this topsy-turvy world view, kindness was covertly avoided and overtly sought at the same time, producing a form of lifetime stress, and an overall introverted personality, but with a high degree of self-reliance due to which he sought never to depend on anyone, and never really quite trusted anyone. Mary's secret cruelties left him with an uncertainty about the unseen dark side of human relations as a somewhat paranoid residual.

Perhaps it should be asked how many men who have had a history of child abuse have undergone this same inversion of personality in which they actually become afraid of kindness, boys who by this inverse pathological route have come to view masculinity as ideally churlish, tough, and cruel, and how many have turned to violence and crime as the ultimate way to proclaim their feelings? Perhaps a compulsive aversion to kindness is one of the hidden prolonged symptoms of a great amount of antisocial behavior that grows out of child abuse.

5

Dan Macdonald's entire life, to date, as noted, had consisted of a long record of small entrepreneurial adventures starting at teenage with a dairy farm, with each new proposition increasing in complication. The odyssey continued during the period of family farm development, when he learned of a greenhouse that was for sale down in Illinois at a place called Niles Center, near Chicago, about a hundred and fifty miles from Montague. The Niles Center area was being incorporated into the city of Chicago, and its previously open farm land subdivided into residential development. The greenhouse, which was to be dismantled to clear the land, was very cheap. To move the structure to Michigan presented Dan with a logistical problem, the building being so far away. But Dan nevertheless got in touch with the owner and arranged a deal. The plan was to carefully disassemble the whole structure, ship it to Montague, and reassemble it on the Macdonald farm.

The greenhouse was not a small structure. It consisted of three interconnected glass houses built side by side, for a total width of ninety feet by two hundred feet long, with a large separate boiler room and potting shed, together with the hot water heating system, irrigation piping, assorted pumps and valves, plus an industrial-sized boiler and smoke stack. Dan, of course, did not have the financial means to pay for an undertaking of this size, so his first job was to talk the local bank manager into financing him.

It was a time of prosperity, so new business undertakings were not difficult to promote, and besides, Dan was very gifted at persuasion. The loan was easily granted, secured by a mortgage on the family farm and home.

John was in the second grade of grammar school at the time, and when the school term ended for the summer vacation, he was surprised to learn that his parents were moving to Niles Center for the summer and John was to accompany them. The other children would remain home and run the farm that summer.

Dan hired a crew of local workmen in Montague, and had them travel to Niles Center and assemble at the greenhouse location, while Dan, Mary, and John drove down there in a new Nash touring car. John remembered the excitement of driving through the Chicago downtown Loop. The year was 1924, and auto traffic was bumper to bumper, moving no faster than a walking pace. There were not yet any traffic signal lights. The traffic was all directed by police officers at each street intersection, using whistles and hand signals amidst much noise and confusion. It took hours to make their way out to Niles Center and the greenhouse site.

The first job was for Mary to set up a temporary boarding house for the workers.

Mary, in addition to being the cook, was also to keep the financial records. Dan set to work organizing the crew and overseeing the job of disassembly, carefully cataloging all for reassembly, and doing it all within the time frame of three months so his children would be free to go back to school in the autumn. Dan was an excellent organizer, and the job proceeded expeditiously. All the various parts were loaded onto freight cars and shipped off to Montague via the Pere Marquette railway. At Montague all was reloaded onto trucks and hauled to Macdonald's farm.

Three items were of interest to John during that summer: first was the efficiency and skill his father exhibited in the monumental undertaking—an entire industrial plant taken apart piece by piece before his eyes, and cataloged for reassembly in Michigan. The second event was a daily air show that was going on overhead. Barnstorm flying entertainment was in vogue then, and each day one or more planes piloted by daring men could be seen performing frightening barrel rolls and tail spins, wing walking, and parachute drops, with each pilot trying to outdo the others in plunging closer to the ground in wild dives before pulling out. The air show went on all summer till one day the planes failed to show up. The newspapers announced sadly that one of the World War I pilots had waited a bit too long to pull out of a spin and had dove right on into terra firma, perhaps a suicide. That was the end of the air show.

The third event that impinged on John's mind concerned black workmen. Sewer and water lines were being installed throughout the Niles Center area in preparation for housing to follow. The ditch-digging was done by hand, using black laborers, but all the foremen were Caucasian. The theory seemed to be that black laborers were to be driven like draft animals, and to do this, the foreman continually shouted very abusive profanity at the workers to urge them on to greater exertion. It was exactly as if the blacks were slaves and were being treated as such, even though slavery had been abolished some sixty years before. As a victim of cruelty himself, John felt a great empathy for these workmen, and even as young as he was, he was appalled at the brutality with which they were treated, and astonished at the indifference exhibited by the local people.

At the Macdonald farm, Dan again displayed his proficiency at reassembling all the disparate parts of this giant jigsaw puzzle of glass, piping, wooden frames, gear-driven ventilators, pumps, valves, boiler, et cetera. The greenhouse was to be adjoined by the boiler room with a deep pit beneath it where the hot water boiler was set up so that convection heat would cause the water to rise and flow without pumping it through the plant heating system. After the reconstruction was finished, Dan bought an overhead oscillating irrigation system to cover the whole farm and a full freight car load of chemical fertilizer to treat the rather infertile Michigan sandy soil.

The greenhouse was a grand idea, and it became an immediate success. Flowers were planted both indoor and out, cultivated, picked, and bunched by the children with the help of a couple of hired employees, packed in ice in shipping boxes, and expressed off to the wholesale market in Chicago where they were distributed to retail florist shops, and they brought gratifying high prices. The money rolled in and the business flourished. But the children began to grumble a bit. Mary prepared their food and kept them on very short rations, and in addition, Dan paid his employees good salaries but gave his kids nothing. Dave was urged to leave school. Dan argued that he was more valuable to the business than the value that his continued education would provide.

Dan's organizing skills and imaginative technology were excellent. His business management was less proficient. He had the bad habit of not doing good accounting, and of letting bills slide by unpaid on time, or sometimes underpaid, or now and again just not paid at all. Payments on the expensive outdoor irrigation system lapsed, probably in spite of good intentions. He seemed to have forgot about paying for the freight car load of fertilizer he had ordered. Even so people put their trust in him because of the enthusiasm with which he could persuade and promote, and inspire confidence. Perhaps his greatest weakness was the passion he had to do things on a grand scale. He never thought in terms of gradualism and working up to a goal. He was too impatient for that.

The economy in 1927 was flourishing and generating lots of new businesses, and the stock market was booming. People were in a jubilant mood. Just at that time, the local newspapers shouted joyously that oil had been discovered in Muskegon County. A rash of drilling started up. Speculative wildcat wells were bored into the swamps of Muskegon Heights, and many of them spewed out high-quality oil in uncontrolled gushers that killed all the plant and animal life within range. Today it would be called an environmental disaster, but in those days, people looked upon it as no more than an inconvenience en route to their dreams of wealth. The appeal to Dan's type of mind, with its penchant for large-scale enterprise and his gamboling optimism, aroused in him a glittering dollar sign fantasy. Dan set to work at once acquiring knowledge of how to form an oil company. He abandoned the greenhouse and florist business to the children and set about rounding up a group of enthusiastic local business people from the Montague area, out of which he organized the White Lake Oil Company.

They sought to raise two hundred thousand dollars by selling unsecured stock to mostly farmers, with the intention of drilling as many wells as they could in their area. The two hundred thousand dollars does not sound like very much money, but considering today's inflated currency, it would probably be the equivalent of two million dollars these decades later.

This was no small enterprise for a man with only a formal third-grade education, although he of course had years of entrepreneurial experience. The challenge of the project fascinated him, and he believed implicitly in the prospects of finding oil. Dan set to work visiting friends, business people, farmers, or anyone who would listen to his proposition and buy a few shares of stock in White Lake Oil Company. To relax inhibitions, both his and the potential stock investor's, he relied upon an easily renewed supply of bootleg whiskey. His enthusiasm and sincerity were contagious, and combined with a little inebriation of both parties, he produced an eager market for the stock. So through hard work and a haze of imbibing, Dan raised the necessary capital to finance the oil company.

Dan located a freelance driller somewhere down in Ohio, by the name of Bill Cook. Dan drove down there, found his man, and struck a deal for drilling as many wells as their capital would pay for. Then over the next couple of years, three wells were bored down to the oil-bearing strata, and each one discouragingly resulted in a dry hole. There was now only enough money left for one last well. The selected site was the back ten acres of Dan's farm. Eureka! It produced oil, but it was only of marginal success due to large incursions of salt water that had to be pumped out of the well with the oil. The oil, however, was an excellent quality of light crude. An electric pump was installed and a receiving tank set up for storage. It seemed that White Lake Oil Company stock was not a total loss, or was it?

Many of the poor farmer investors in the White Lake Oil Company began grumbling and Dan's reputation as a businessman in the community was eroded somewhat. But Dan himself continued with an attitude of unabated enthusiasm for the future. Increasingly though his alcoholic binges with his friends began to usurp his energy, with the consequence of a lack of attention to the farm. Productivity began to decline even while the economy was still flourishing. Sister Helen began taking on more and more of the responsibility of running the business before she was out of high school. Brother Dave's labor was farmed out to customers for landscape gardening work, and Dan took whatever salary he earned and gave him nothing in return but inadequate food and clothing. It was a form of paternal slavery to which Dave, a docile and obendient son, although grumbling, acceded. Tragically he never returned to school. Dan, having little education himself, had little understanding and awareness of the ever-increasing complexity of life and therefore lacked a vision of the expanding need of education for his children.

The oil drilling procedure was fascinating to John, and every chance he got, he would visit the site of the Macdonald well as it was being literally hammered down into the bedrock below. This was before the time of rotary drilling technology. The drill bit consisted of a long steel shaft that was perhaps eight inches in diameter and probably weighed several tons.

It had a short chisel-shaped boring bit that was threaded onto the main assembly so that it could be removed for sharpening. The heavy drilling tool with its steel chisel end was lowered into the well casing pipe by means of a steel cable that unwound from a so-called "bull wheel." The bull wheel consisted of a massive wooden winch that was about eight feet in diameter, and was driven by a donkey steam engine, using coal for fuel. When the drilling assembly was let down into the bottom of the well at the end of its long cable, a giant walking beam then gripped the cable and the steam engine applied power to produce an up-and-down plunging movement of the drill while workmen twisted the cable to keep the bit turning at the end of the suspension cable.

Slowly, hour after hour, the up and down movement of the heavy drill with its constant rotation, working in water at the bottom of the well, ground out a shaft of bedrock to ever deeper depths. After a few feet of drilling was accomplished, the bit was hoisted to the surface and a bailer was lowered down the well to gather up the ground-up rock sludge and remove it to the surface to be discarded in a sludge pond. When it was judged that the drill bit had become too dull to proceed, the drilling assembly was hoisted from the well and the boring bit was unscrewed and placed in a forge and brought to a white heat. The bit was then laid out on a huge anvil to be sharpened. Two well-muscled men stripped to the waist, and wielding heavy sledgehammers, beat out the chisel end of the bit to a renewed sharp edge, using an easy contrapuntal rhythm so that it was like watching dancers perform.

The bit was then reheated to a glowing cherry red and plunged into a barrel of cold water to set the temper of the steel, then reattached onto the full drilling assembly, to continue pounding away at the bedrock below in a slow repetitive process. Bill Cook had cleverly arranged a drilling contract by the hour of drilling time rather than by the foot of depth, so he was in no hurry to get the job done.

After the Macdonald well was brought into limited production, the company decided to "blow the well in," with the hope that it would increase the yield. The practice was to lower a large quantity of explosive down the shaft to the oil-bearing strata and set off the charge to break up the rock so that oil might flow more freely into the well cavity. This was a job for a specialist, and for a man with iron nerves, for the explosive they used was pure nitroglycerin. The fluid was cooled to its lowest possible temperature by the primitive refrigeration available at that time, and then transported to the well by a soft riding automobile. There were no laws to prevent the frighteningly dangerous explosive from being driven over public highways and through downtown areas.

On the day that the nitroglycerin arrived at the Macdonald well, John, who had been visiting the drilling operation daily, dropped by to see how things were going. For some reason that he didn't understand, the doors of the drilling shed were closed.

He was surprised because they had never been closed before. No one seemed to be around. John opened the door and there before him was a man pouring an oily-looking liquid, from what looked like a five-gallon milk can, into a tubular container. The man looked up but continued to pour and said in a very gentle calm voice, "Get the hell out of here, kid." John quietly shut the door and retreated about a quarter of a mile.

After the explosive was lowered gently down the well to the proper depth, it was followed by a time fuse attached to a detonator cap to explode the charge. In the event that the detonator failed to work, a second impaction device, called a "go devil," consisting of a suspended weight, could be released by remote means, which would then plunge down the well, hit the charge, and set it off.

On the day of the "blowing in" procedure, there was a gathering of the stockholders, attentive but stoically glum, to watch the last capital from their failed investment discharged in a big explosion at the bottom of a marginal oil well. Everyone understood that the results of this last effort would determine the success or utter failure of the White Lake Oil Company. Dan seemed unworried, for he loved the excitement of setting off a massive explosion. It was akin to his attraction to using dynamite.

When the nitro exploded, a huge quantity of rock slurry, water, and some oil ejected out of the well, plummeting over the top of the derrick. John was thrilled by the results, but oddly there was not much accompanying sound from the explosion, though there was an impressive trembling of the earth he stood upon. And sure enough, when they began pumping oil again, they found the shattered rock strata did somewhat increase the oil production.

All of this oil business had a great appeal to Dan. He loved the drama of it—gamboling chance taking and explosive charges; his was an active and experimental vitality. Unfortunately he also had a rather scant sense of caution with his propensity for experimentation, characteristics that could combine to produce some spectacular events. One day he decided to do something about the slurry pond that had been formed when the oil well was drilled. It had become scummed over with tarry oil and was trapping birds, and it looked nasty. Dan decided to burn it off to clean it up. He applied for and got a burn permit from the fire department, but due to his usual aura of self-confidence, they didn't inquire too much about what he was going to burn. He first tried to start a flame with matches, but the tarry substance refused to ignite. It was clear that more heat would be required, so he built a little bonfire on the surface of the pond. Nothing much happened, except the tar began to melt. Suddenly the entire pond erupted in an explosive inferno.

Within seconds the flames were leaping about thirty feet in the air and sending immense clouds of dense black smoke billowing up hundreds of feet. The towering smoke column could be seen miles away. The fire department responded with all the equipment they possessed, but the heat was so intense that they couldn't get near enough to use water to quench it. The pump shed ignited and burned up. The oil storage tank, filled to capacity with thousands of gallons of crude oil, was in imminent danger. But suddenly as quickly as the fire had grown to its terrifying size, it receded and burned out, leaving a nice clean gray slurry pond that could be filled in with earth. Dan was very pleased with the results and dismissed the fire as a minor event that had got the job done just right.

The greenhouse was heated by a large coal-burning furnace that during the cold Michigan winters became a slave driver to stoke. Day and night, through the long winter, someone had to shovel coal fast enough into the furnace to keep the temperature above freezing for the plants, shake down and rake out the clinkers, haul away ash, haul tons of coal from the coal shed in a wheelbarrow, and dump it down into the furnace pit while constantly monitoring temperature. Much of this work, if not most of it, was delegated by Dan, for Dave to do at about age sixteen. He had been taken out of school to work at home.

The coal, which was purchased by the freight car load, was a very burdensome expense. Dan pondered the problem and came up with another new idea. Without consulting the White Lake Oil Company stockholders, he piped oil from the Macdonald well across the Coon Creek cow pasture over to the greenhouse, and converted the furnace to burn crude oil. Along the route of the pipeline, Dan built a crude distilling plant that was intended to draw off the volatile gasoline from the high-quality crude oil, and this fuel would then be used to operate the farm tractor and truck. It was just the sort of inventive idea that Dan loved to devise. But his technology was not as advanced as his imagination. Again there was a magnificent explosion and fire when the distilling plant blew sky high. Fortunately, no one was near it at the time. Dan brushed off the explosion with a mere shrug, for he had learned that the crude oil had so much gasoline in it that with a simple piping grid, it would form so-called "drip gas," which could be drained off for the truck and tractor. The gasoline acquired by this method was so volatile that the tractor could be started with a flip of the ignition switch in the coldest weather.

The burning of oil to heat the greenhouse was a triumphant success, and the fuel was free except for the cost of pumping it. It should have given Dan a great financial advantage over his competition in the nursery business, but by this time he was becoming ever more dependent on alcohol and the business was ever more neglected.

6

During the years of development of the Macdonalds' farm and the White Lake Oil Company, the Spartan life went on as usual in the Macdonald home, and now Dan was staying away from home more and more, seeking out his drinking companions. Often he would only show up at the farm long enough to tell the children what work he wanted them to carry out. Dan's absences didn't bother Mary any, for it gave her a free rein to rule the children in her own way, and she took full advantage of being the head of the family to inflect her hostility on them.

Perhaps the most dispiriting effect on the personalities of all the children was caused by the severe ritual of eating meals together. The children were intimidated and were prohibited from speaking during meals except to respond to questions or to utter a subdued "Thank you" when food was served to them. Everyone in the family sat down together for meals at an old oak table in the kitchen, and each child had his own chair and his own place at the table that never varied. John sat next to his stepmother on her left. From this handy proximity, Mary could reach over to slap him on the side of the face or box his ears with an open palm whenever she felt inclined to do so, and her inclinations were all too frequent. Sitting next to her and anticipating that he could be struck at any time without warning set up a state of dread and worry. She would begin the attack by an angry order such as, "Stop bolting your food!" WHAM!

Bolting meant eating too fast.

When one is semi-starving, it is difficult to refrain from bolting food down, so Mary had an ongoing excuse to strike at any time. Mary served each child a plate of food and carefully measured the amount commensurate to age, but unfortunately no child ever got enough to satisfy an appetite, and they were forbidden to ask for more. The children ate in subdued silence. There was only conversation carried on at the dinner table during those infrequent times when Dan was home to eat with them, and then the conversation excluded the children and was confined to Dan and Mary discussing prosaic matters. Dan, at these times, was served very different food from that which the children received. He feasted on steaks, or bacon and eggs, and ham, and special menus of smoked fish while the children were served a bland bowl of oatmeal each. Dan did not seem to notice that he was producing drooling envy on the part of the children. Apparently he assumed that as head of the family, it was his prerogative to have an imperial separate menu.

The net result of this state of malnutrition was that the children learned to steal food at every opportunity—from their own pantry, from the garden and orchards, from other farmers' orchards and gardens, and even from the stores. Dan bought up stale moldy bread from a bakery to be fed to the chickens. It was stored, under lock and key, in his and Mary's bedroom.

Whenever their parents were not at home, the children, who had secretly acquired a key, would enter the room and gorge themselves on moldy doughnuts. Chronic hunger was such an everlasting condition in the children's lives that it became an obsession for them to search for food everywhere—wild sour grass was eaten, wild strawberries, wintergreen berries and leaves. The Michigan woods produced quantities of huckleberries in the autumn and the children browsed on them.

The children were always hungry and at times devised interesting food supplements. Once a year the Pepsodent Toothpaste Company handed out little samples of toothpaste to the children at school for advertising. John and brother Ron always ate the toothpaste on the way home from school, but of course, John was never given a toothbrush anyway.

The children's everlasting gnawing hunger sharpened their wits to seek out like cunning animals sources of food whenever and wherever an opportunity arose. Perhaps their greatest cornucopia was found when the local Ornaburger's Grocery and Meat Market burned. The fire gutted the inside of the building, but most of the canned food was unspoiled, in spite of all the labels being burned off the cans. The walk-in refrigerator had strings of sausages looped across the room and whole hams hung from meat hooks unspoiled.

For the purpose of a long-delayed insurance inspection, everything in the market was left as it was after the fire, and the building was boarded up. The Macdonald children, with great joy, found a way into the back of the store and hauled away as much canned food as they could throughout about a week of time, and secretly cached it for the future. With no labels to go by, it was always a delightful surprise to open a can of food and find out what you had. It was one of the few times in John's childhood that he had enough food to still the pangs of hunger.

At that time lard was sold in little half-gallon tin buckets, with a wire handle and press on lids. The pails were quite handy to use after the lard was consumed, and Mary kept them for school lunch pails. John's school lunch consisted of one slice of bread cut through the middle, spread thinly with peanut butter, and the other half-slice completing the sandwich. Year after year neither the amount nor the menu varied. Mary gave no consideration to the fact that John was growing and needed an increase in rations from time to time. At noon John would gobble down his scanty lunch and then watch other children as they ate their envied lunches of ham sandwiches, boiled eggs, cookies and cake, and all sorts of things that made John drool. Occasionally to help satisfy his hunger, John would steal an apple or a banana off of the teacher's desk, food that had been given to her by a student, then hide in the cloak room and bolt the food down.

Holidays were looked forward to with hungry anticipation by the children. There were two holidays in the year, Christmas and Thanksgiving, and occasionally a third holiday, Independence Day. On these days the children could expect a larger than normal ration of food when Mary's two sisters and their husbands would all have dinner at the Macdonalds' farm house. Part of the holiday pleasure, for John, was that during holiday meals he could feel reasonably confident that he wouldn't be slapped in the face during the meal.

Mary was an excellent cook, but it was only on these rare holiday occasions when there were visiting relatives, that the children had any chance to appreciate her skill. The typical holiday meal consisted of a prime rooster from the poultry yard, whose head was chopped off in the back yard with an ax, plucked, stuffed with dressing, and roasted to a golden perfection in the kitchen wood stove oven. The chicken would be accompanied by homemade bread rolls, mashed potatoes with chicken gravy, steamed Hubbard squash mashed and buttered, and occasionally a home-canned green vegetable like green beans or peas, with the meal topped off by a homemade apple pie with apples from the apple barrel in the back yard.

During the holiday meal, the children, as usual sat rigid and in complete silence while the adults conversed. It was always understood by the children, that they had no right to speak unless spoken to.

Lucy's husband, Uncle Elmer, was a gifted raconteur, and John was entranced by his table stories. He would launch into a narrative with a preliminary clicking of his dentures, followed by a wheezing and sucking of air around his partially dislodged teeth, and then onward with "A fellow told me...," and a long delightful story would follow with lurid details and graphic hyperbole, building always toward a triumphant climax that was drawn out to excite the anticipation of the listener. It was much better than television at its best.

The Montague community projected a mild aura of innocence in the jazzy age of speak-easy bistros and flapper dancing, and there was just a bit of clannish rebuff of the Chicago city slickers who came to the village to spend their summer vacations, with their bulging billfolds. Whitehall, the adjoining town at the other end of the lake, was slightly larger than Montague and perhaps a little less provincial. The two towns provided each other with a competitive foil to challenge one another in sporting duels of football and baseball. Montague had the best deep-water docking facilities on White Lake, and a passenger ship of the Goodrich Company plied back and forth between Chicago and Montague during the summer tourist season. It was an annual ritual to welcome the first voyage of the ship following the breakup of the winter lake ice and the coming of school vacations. Spring had arrived when the vessel's bass steam whistle carried across the lake to the village shore.

With festive anticipation, the local people gathered to

watch her glide into her mooring. She was fetching the summer vacationers with their luxury dollars. Shortly the beaches would be spotted with gaily colored sun umbrellas and populated with young ladies from the city, wearing the newest and most daring low-necked bathing suits, but with skirts that reached almost to the knees. Young men promenaded in their latest attire too, a full body suit with a sun hole on each side under the arm at rib cage level. Most men were far too modest for bathing trunks and an exposed bare chest.

As the summer warmed the village and all the oaks and maples grew plush with mantles of green leaves, the watermelons and tree-ripened fruit gorged with sweet juices appeared in the markets after a long winter, a happy gaiety spread through the Montague populace that found its expression in a town carnival or perhaps a circus, or a Memorial Day parade and balloon ascension, or even a dance at the lake pavilion to the strains of a jazz orchestra.

It is difficult to treat children so severely that some natural ebullience of spirit does not break forth fed by the sheer vitality of summer combined with being young. With the charming town of Montague as a backdrop for their youth, the Macdonald children were animated to break free from their tensions of chronic hunger and irrational discipline and abuse by "Ma."

Also the common enemy caused the children to draw together in a common bond to support each other in finding niches of happiness and entertainment. The combined abuse and pastoral beneficence of the little village created a gourmet life of sweet and sour for John, a heightened blend that sharpened awareness.

The highlight of the summer was the Fourth of July Independence Day. Even Dan took part in the exploding activities. On this happy day, firecrackers, as noise makers, were too weak a response. Dan had his own special passion for dynamite, and he always had a box or two around the house. His endorsement of Independence Day was to hang a stick of dynamite from a limb of the front yard oak tree and proudly set it off first thing in the morning with an ear-splitting "BANG," which rattled the windows in Whitehall across the lake.

The children had little access to firecrackers, so brother Dave fell back on his own inventive talent. From the hardware stores, calcium carbide was readily available, a compound that produces acetylene gas when combined with water. At that time, as noted, lard was sold in little tin pails with a press-on lid. Dave purchased a few cents worth of carbide, and the kids each acquired a lard bucket from the town dump. A small hole was punctured in the bottom of the bucket and a piece of carbide tossed into it. The boys then spit on the carbide to wet it, then sealed the top with the press-on lid.

Lightly stepping on the bucket to hold it in place, a match was touched to the bottom punched hole, and the gas exploded with a gratifying "Bang!" and blew the cover off. The same bucket and piece of carbide could be used over and over again to bang away all day for a dime.

July in Michigan could produce her own fireworks, midsummer days that came on hot and humid, and so still you became sharply aware of the buzz of bottle flies and the whirring sound of grasshopper wings, and then a billowing up of black thunderhead clouds. Suddenly an electric flash and the long-echoed roll of thunder that introduced a quick shower and the odor of ozone. Pizzicato raindrops rattled the summer corn husks, and every tree and plant plumed their leaves and blossoms. Summer rains dissolved as quickly as they were born, leaving behind a clean, green, verdant earth.

Summer rains were the reveille call for Michigan wildflowers, and a time for Dan to pack the children into the Nash touring car and drive out into the countryside to have the kids gather armloads of lupines, goldenrod, and black-eyed Susan daisies. The carload of flowers was wetted to keep them fresh, and hurried home where the children stripped their bottom leaves, gathered them in bunches, packed them in ice, and shipped them off to the Chicago floral market. Both the labor and the flowers were free, so it was a highly profitable business for Dan.

On one of these wildflower gathering occasions, Dan ran across a lovely bed of bright yellow mushrooms that especially appealed to his esthetic sensibilities. Making a quick judgment, he thought anything that attractive must be good to eat, so he gathered a large box of them and brought them home. But then caution overcame his first impression, and casting about for a way to test their eatableness, it occurred to him that there was a voracious variety of slugs that had gotten into the greenhouse in a shipment of plants, and they would be the ideal creatures to test the viability of the mushrooms for human consumption. So Dan placed some slugs and yellow mushrooms in a box together and left them overnight. Checking out the experiment next morning, he found that sure enough, the slugs had eaten the yellow mushrooms. The fact that the slugs were almost all dead escaped his notice. After all, slugs were not really like people.

So he had Mary cook up the whole box of mushrooms for a gourmet dinner for the children. Mary did not eat any, perhaps motivated by caution, and Dan, a finicky eater, left the house to attend to his own affairs. Less than an hour after the meal was consumed, all the children were sick and vomiting. It was one of those rare occasions in their family life when a physician was called. She diagnosed it as acute poisoning that was so severe it had caused immediate reactive vomiting that expelled the poison before it became fatal. Dan didn't concern himself too much about poisoning the children, and shrugged off the incident. After all, he reasoned, all life is eventually terminal.

One day while Dan was driving out into the country with the kids on a Sunday adventure, he ran across a dump site where a canning factory had dumped an entire truckload of canned fruit that had spoiled. All the cans were bulged out from the internal pressure of the gas that had formed in them. Dan immediately got a bright new idea. He loaded the car with all the fruit cans he could pack in between the children and headed for home with great excitement. At home he set to work down in the cellar constructing a homemade distillery. His idea was to heat the cans just enough to vaporize the alcohol, then condense the vapors through a copper tubing coil back into a sort of fruit brandy. The still was pretty crude, so the amount of alcohol that was produced was only the most volatile condensate.

With great enthusiasm Dan introduced the fruit brandy to his drinking pals. It was so powerful that they only warily sipped at it. They were impressed by the fire of the concoction, and certainly by his technology, but again everyone got violently ill except Dan. His drinking cronies thereafter went back to their good wholesome bootleg suppliers, and Dan's reputation as a distiller was tarnished somewhat, but they loved him for his ardor and good fellowship.

Brother Dave, seven years older than John, had a talent like his father's for invention that gave rise to numerous forms of creativity from dug-out dens to water wheels.

Behind the greenhouse was a little fenced-in pasture through which Coon Creek wandered on its way to emptying into White Lake. Topsy, the Macdonald cow, had her pasture there, wallowed in the bogs, and peacefully munched watercress. Dave decided it was the ideal place to build an earth dam, with an overflow that would run a water wheel. The children all participated in the construction, and soon a quarter acre pond extended upstream that quickly became populated with polliwogs and fat bullfrogs. To add to the scene, Dave built a model ship, which cruised the miniature marine world. It became a gathering spot for the village kids, where like Topsy they could wallow in the mud too, and where they could pursue frogs and pole a raft up and down the pond.

Downstream from the pond was a hillside of oak woods. Here, whenever the opportunity occurred, Dave directed the boys in carving out a secret den in the side of the hill, walled it in with old boards, and roofed it over with corrugated tin covered with soil for camouflage. Dave invented a special combination lock to thwart intruders, and into the dugout structure, the children moved an old discarded cook stove and various crude benches and chairs. It became a club house gathering place for friends and a refuge from adult scrutiny. The fun thing to do was to raid a village garden for sweet corn, or someone's orchard for apples, and bring the loot to the dugout.

There a fire was built in the stove, and soon they could serve themselves roasted corn with baked apples in a camaraderie of gossip and jokes.

Among the children's friends, who shared the hideaway, was a lad who had a twelve-gauge shotgun. One day while the gang was enjoying an afternoon in the dugout baking apples and corn, the shotgun-wielding youngster quietly approached outside and tossed a handful of shotgun shells down the stove chimney. Without warning all the stove lids blew off, the oven door blasted open, and black soot and apples shrapneled through the room. The confined sound of the explosion was deafening. The kids bolted for the door in a knot of bodies. Outside the boys wiped the soot from their faces and clothes, and after making sure no one was hurt, they exploded in gales of laughter.

Sometimes in summer, after the children's assigned work was done, Dan would allow brother Dave to crank up the Model-T Ford farm truck and drive all the children out to Lake Michigan for a romp on the beach. It was only a few miles, but it seemed to John like a vast expedition charged with excitement and adventure. The rutted dirt road out to Lake Michigan divided farms and traced right angles around green hay fields and about apple orchards, and wound through hickory and maple woods. At last the road ended in a lush pine grove at the back side of a sugary white sand dune where Dave parked the steaming, rattling vehicle.

Everyone dashed out and up to the top of the dune to behold the Great Lake sparking in undulating gentle waves against miles of pristine white shoreline, and without a single man-made structure anywhere to violate its far horizons of natural beauty.

Michigan seasons were decisive and distinctly different from each other, not like the leisurely changes of tropical climates to the south. When autumn came there was a hurrying of growth, acorns forming, maples seeding, grapes swelling with purple juice, apples blushing with bright colors, all the maturing fruits and vegetables swelling rapidly to nourish the population for the coming winter, all hurrying to complete the growing cycle before all were destroyed by the first snow. Village kitchens were a beehive of activity with women filling canning jars, or making pickles, or boiling jams and jellies.

As the nights turned colder and the deciduous tree

leaves burnished red and gold, and then fell to the ground in a carpet of umber, it was time to anticipate the coming of winter and all that it entailed: getting in a supply of coal, slaughtering the hogs and packing their dismembered bodies into the smoke house for preservation, stowing a barrel of apples in the ground in the back yard covered with straw for insulation, digging the potatoes and carrots and placing them in the cellar for winter storage. For the Macdonald children, it was a time of hard hyperactivity, all of it directed by Dan.

For elderly people winter at White Lake was a cold threat; for the children it was an enchantment that inspired anticipation of a seven-mile skating rink that formed when the lake iced over. The ice thickness varied from year to year, from a few inches to as much as eighteen inches in an especially cold winter. New ice that sets up quickly during a cold snap is thin, but tough and flexible. It is extremely dangerous and even foolhardy to skate on it. But for those who are crazy enough to do it, the trick is to skate fast so that the body weight never remains in one place long enough to break through.

Brother Ron, always daring and disposed to rash behavior, like his father, was usually the first person to try out the new ice. The ice could be as little as two inches thick when Ron would skip school, clamp on a pair of skates over thick-soled work shoes (for fancy shoe skates were beyond the means of most village children), and venture out onto the ice. The first order of the day was to check out the near shore ice for quality and weight bearing. If it appeared to pass the test, Ron would shoulder his homemade skate sail, catch the wind on a quartering tack, and head out across the lake at twenty to thirty miles an hour. He reveled in beating the highway traffic as cars drove along the lake shore road. The rubbery ice might bend down beneath his weight, but he passed over it so fast that it didn't break. It was dangerous and foolhardy. If he had a guardian angel, she must have been fully occupied looking after him.

Since no one else dared to accompany him, he had the lake all to himself.

On a Saturday morning with a bright winter sun and good safe skating ice, the lake would be a beehive of activity, with several hundred people out on the ice to enjoy the day. There would be amateur hockey games played with home-carved clubs and a block of wood for a puck; there were homemade ice boats, a T-framed structure with sled runners and a seat, mast, and triangular sails; and there were dozens of boys with their own individual skate sails. Fishermen cut holes in the ice and placed set lines with a little flag that tipped up when the fish tugged on the line. Other fishermen pushed little skid-mounted fish shanties out on the ice. Inside the fish shanty, a small block of ice was cut out and removed to fish through. The fisherman sat in his cozy little dark room with the sun shining through the ice on the outside, and when a big pike or bass passed across the fisherman's view, enticed by a bright-colored moving lure made of yarn, the fisherman plunged a barbed spear into his quarry and retrieved fish and spear with an attached line.

The local ice company sent a crew out onto the ice-covered lake with a wagon sled drawn by a team of horses. The men, equipped with special ice saws, cut out squares of ice weighing about fifty pounds each.

With giant tongs the block ice was loaded onto the sled to be drawn back to the village ice house where the blocks were stacked indoors and covered with sawdust, to be sold the following summer from door to door to the local residents. A story was told of a team of horses breaking through the ice and coming up under the glassy sheet to be watched in horror as the animals struggled hopelessly and drowned.

After the sun went down and darkness of evening approached, skaters were reluctant to leave the lake ice. Across the lake was a large tanning factory called the Eagle-Attawa Tanning Works. Tannic acid was purchased by them in wooden barrels, and over the years, it had become a custom for the village boys to steal the empty barrels and adapt them to their own use. After dark a raiding party would be organized to skate to the tannery where a small group of boys would start a diversionary noisy disturbance at one side of the factory to attract the watchmen, and a larger group would skate to the other side where the barrels were stored, and roll dozens of them out onto the lake ice. The tops and bottoms of the barrels were knocked out, and a small bonfire was started on the ice, for which there was no danger of a melt-through because the ice was too thick. The barrels were then stacked on top of one another as high as possible to form a chimney over the fire. Quickly the draft would carry the flames up through the barrels to form a magnificent torch light in the center of the lake.

Around this lake center beacon, children and townspeople skated arm in arm in a grand finale to cap off the day of skating.

Skiing was only beginning to become a popular sport, and it inspired brother Dave to try his skill at making homemade skis. The difficult part was the sled runner curve in the toe of the skis. The usual way to form this curve was to steam the wood under low pressure till it became pliable enough to bend. The hand-shaped ski is then removed from the steam bath, quickly bent over a form, and held in place till the wood dries. The bend is then permanent. The bend has to be somewhat greater than required to allow for the tendency of the wood to spring back after it is released from the form, so it becomes a matter of good judgment as to how much it must be bent, and of course too much will break the wood. Dave made a steamer for his lumber out of a length of large diameter pipe. After steaming the skis were given their final shape and leather foot straps added, then bright painted pin striping and multiple coats of varnish, with a final coat of beeswax on the bottoms. They were rather primitive, but John thought they were beautiful, and they did serve their purpose very well.

Most skiing was of the cross-country variety because the Montague area had few good hills for ski runs.

A favorite weekend sport for the boys was to request from Dan the use of the family twenty-two caliber rifle, don skis, and tour the back country looking for fresh rabbit tracks in a new fallen snow. Tracks leading into a shock of last season's corn could often lead to flushing out a rabbit, if the shock was given a kick. With a combination of luck and skill, the boys often provided themselves with a private feast in their dug-out den to supplement the scant rations at home.

Dan had a curious lack of caution about life in general—when for example, he allowed the children to freely roam the countryside with a gun with very little previous instruction or supervision. They were daily set to work operating farm machinery, truck and tractor, and even the family car with the scantiest of training. But however dangerous their exposure to machinery and tools was, it had a lifelong advantageous effect, for it exposed them to learning all sorts of work skills and tool use that few sheltered children ever get.

The machinery that Dan installed at the Macdonald farm was wholly in keeping with his penchant for lack of caution, all of it bereft of guards or safety features of any kind. A series of drive belts for water pumps and motors in the boiler room operated in the open with not even a guard rail. Brother Ron, while playing tag one day, excitedly lost his balance near an operating pump. Instinctively he threw his hand out to catch himself and grasped the moving belt.

It lifted him quickly to the ceiling of the building, and just before the moving belt could throw him over the top of the pulley, Ron let go and landed barefoot on top of an oil can spout, driving it through his foot. He pulled it out of his foot himself and it eventually healed without medical attention. It never would have occurred to Dan to have a doctor look at it, but it must be said that Dan was equally careless of his own safety, and his neglect was not selfishly motivated; it was just born of indifference. Daily Dan carried a box of dynamite around in his rough-riding Nash touring car over pot-holed farm roads while kindly picking up hitch-hiking riders. When they spied the open box of dynamite sticks jolting up and down in the car, they would blanch white, and ask politely if they could go their own way on foot. Dan thought it was very amusing.

It was a family rule that the boys should always go barefoot during the summer to save shoes for attending school. It developed tough healthy feet, but often exposed them to many accidental cuts from broken glass and nail-studded boards around the farm buildings. Rarely were such injuries ever reported to their parents, and if they had been, they would have been ignored anyway. Medical attention was looked upon as an unnecessary luxury. The occasional physical injuries and childhood diseases were dismissed as just part of the normal experience of growing up.

In late autumn the boys were still going barefoot, even while the brisk early mornings produced fields white with frost. One of the morning chores was to take the Macdonalds' cow Topsy, after milking, to her pasture, about a mile distant. The white frost on bare feet was a painful experience at this time. Fortunately, after Topsy had been in the barn overnight, she was moved to evacuate her bowels en route to the pasture, and the boys could hardly wait for it to happen so they could run and immerse their feet in the pliant warm pile of manure to warm their feet.

One of the rituals in the Macdonald family, when school was starting in the autumn, was for Mary to cut the boys' hair so close that you could see their scalps. As a barber, Mary was not too particular about steps and gouges as long as it was short. The hair-cutting was accompanied by such other activities as donning shoes again and sorting out hand-me-down clothing. John was distressed at returning to school, for he was ashamed of his appearance. Mary made his school clothes out of discarded adult clothing, and she had a set pattern that remained the same year after year, which may have been quite popular in the days of Charles Dickens. It consisted of a sailor middy and suspendered short trousers bloused and elasticized at the knees, with long black stockings and button shoes. All the other boys were wearing long trousers with neat shirts and jackets, and laced shoes, and were neatly shorn by a skilled barber.

When John was asked to stand and recite before the class, he would wilt with humiliation. Inevitably the lasting result of his shame was that he shrank from socializing and became introverted and a poor student. His relief valve was reading, and he became an avid reader. While other students were playing at lunchtime, he was engrossed in encyclopedias and the exploits of Madame Curie's radium separation or the current theories of atomic particles, and he loved science fiction, especially the stories of Jules Verne.

If his learning could have been relieved of inhibitions, he would have become an excellent student. As it was, distractions by home environment, embarrassment about clothing and appearance, and suffering from chronic hunger, resulted in such low self-esteem that he was an abysmal student.

But John's public school experience was not all distressing. With the passage of time and the occasional interdiction of his father on his behalf, he was being given more freedom to join schoolmates in their social activities. One such event left a lifetime nostalgic memory. John was in the fifth grade. His teacher was Mrs. Storms, and notwithstanding her name, she was a warm, motherly schoolmarm under whose tutelage John did his best work. His class planned a horse-drawn sleighing party. On the appointed evening, the children gathered at Mrs. Storms's house. It was a picture-postcard moonlit night, and the countryside was covered with fresh deep snow.

The sleigh appeared, drawn by a team of horses bedecked with ribbons and bells. In those days the farmers converted their farm wagons into sleighs during the winter by removing the wheels and mounting the wagon bed on sleigh runners. The wagon bed was filled with loose fresh straw, and into it tumbled the class of perhaps twenty children.

The horses started off at a bell-jingling trot along the village streets, and Mrs. Storms started a round of songs to which the children added their combined voices. They traveled the country roads for a rollicking couple of hours, and then back to the teacher's house for a finale of hot chocolate. To John's mind there never could have been a more delightful adventure than that horse-drawn sleigh ride in a snow-covered countryside on a moonlit night in 1927. The memory of it lasted a lifetime. The importance of an event, such as the sleigh ride, is not determined by the magnitude of the event itself, but by the penury of living in which it is couched.

7

John thought of himself as a good child, if he thought of it at all, but that thinking was limited to the moral system that he thought goodness meant. Under the authoritarianism of his stepmother, it obviously meant to carry out exactly whatever he was ordered to do, even if the orders seemed arbitrary and irrational. It meant above all that to be good was to have almost no right to free thought and action. Self-volition was a vice contrary to goodness and subject to severe punishment in his diminished world of authoritarianism. Consequently, when he got into grammar school where children were expected to make free choices and achieve gradations of rightness, where school lessons could be partly right and partly wrong, and were then graded fairly on the margin of error or of success, his attitude of obeisance and submission that had developed at home left him fearful, confused, and diffident in school.

John's struggle with arithmetic exemplified the trouble he had. He could not understand the relationship between numbers or the code for adding or subtracting. His arithmetic papers were always marked completely wrong. It was a devastating experience because, given his terror of being bad, for which he could be punished at home, he struggled endlessly to find some way to get the right answers to the arithmetic problems. Then one day he discovered that the girl who sat in front of him always had the right answers. It was obvious that all he had to do was to copy her papers.

His grades miraculously improved.

He felt gratified in having worked out a way of reducing his worry. It was immaterial to him how he got the right answers to arithmetic problems, for in all of his early school years, his self-image of success was dependent upon lowering the threshold of concern that he would be verbally punished if he did not come up to an acceptable level of scholastic competence. It is said that "Sticks and stones can break your bones, but words can never hurt you," but this adage is not true. Verbal punishment, such as accusations of stupidity, are as cruel as corporal punishment, and probably longer lasting. With his warped view of being good as the coequivalent of not being labeled as stupid, together with his terror of being punished for being bad, it was perfectly logical to copy other students' papers. The teacher moved him to another seat behind an equally bad math student. John was dumfounded and puzzled. Why was he moved when he was doing so well sitting behind the bright student?

Only gradually did he come to understand that the object of math was not only to get the right answers, but to also get them by the right calculation. He never became a good math student, but it measurably lowered his fear of punishment to find that if he was wrong in an answer, it was not the same as being bad. Eventually he became fascinated with the orderly relationship of numbers, while discovering that school was not like home; you could be partially successful without the cold fear of reprisal.

Early in John's life, a conflict of values brought about inner tensions that no adult could ever be aware of. Integrity, courage, and rectitude were the themes of the books he read, novels by Horatio Alger, Robert Louis Stevenson, Zane Grey . . . novels whose characters displayed heroic courage in their adventures, thwarting evil and displaying virtues wherein good people inevitably triumphed in the finale. He was deeply impressed and emotionally moved by literature. But the literature-inculcated idealism was set against a backdrop of necessity for him to steal food to supplement his scanty rations at home. To complicate matters, Dan and Mary sent the children to Sunday school to learn religion, but they did not attend church themselves, and often a favorite table conversation for Dan was to proclaim his low regard for ministers and lawyers. Ministers were lazy parasites living off the community, and lawyers were outright scoundrels. His polemics on the subject were frequent and loud, goaded as he was by an alcoholic lack of inhibition.

John was confused with the reason for going to Sunday school when ministers of the church were of such questionable morality. Adding to the complicated moral construct that was evolving in John's mind was that his stepmother, Mary, pictured God as a monstrous force whose central function was to punish. Mary did not seem to make a self-connecting evaluation, or question her own behavior. Apparently she and God were buddies.

Mary's view of religion tended to embrace a vast file of superstitions about every imaginable subject from astrology to reading tea leaves.

John's Sunday school class was held in the basement of the church, a dark damp vault of a place. The Sunday school teacher glowingly emphasized the miracles of God and read to the children long scriptural passages from the Bible. While John was dozing off, he often raised his eyes to a dimly lighted colored wall poster of a feminine-looking Christ, a very un-Jewish Anglo-Saxon blond who was levitating up through the clouds and sun rays, presumably on his way to heaven, rising up and away from the carnal humanity that had rejected his message. The general gloom of the tomb-like room together with the dreary readings, the dubious miracle of ascension, and the confused religious views of his parents, all combined to produce superstitious fears and doubts and a lasting cynicism.

John puzzled and speculated endlessly about religion; was the Bible story really the truth or was it just a story? Was God an omnipotent being who knew about John's sin of stealing food? Would he be punished for it? And what did God look like? John never arrived at any really satisfactory answers, and his quandary may be expressed by an event that happened one day on his way to Sunday school.

It was a lovely Michigan day with bracing air, modulated by bird songs. The thought of the damp, dark basement Sunday school class, presided over by a dreary-voiced teacher droning on and on reading Scriptures that he never understood, and the unconvincing picture of Jesus defying gravity raised an uncharacteristic spirit of rebellion in John. What a lark it would be, he speculated, to take his three pennies, which he had been provided for the collection plate, and which he was always ashamed of because of the niggardly amount, take them to the village drug store, buy candy, and forget the Sunday school class. It was a daring notion and he was not usually given to such evil ideas. If found out, his punishment could be dreadful, and there was the added worry, what would God do to him? But the idea overwhelmed his sense of caution, and he forthwith took himself downtown to the drug store and skipped Sunday school.

At that time, about 1923, Michigan allowed slot machines to be placed in stores, and Ripley's Drug Store, which also sold candy and ice cream, displayed a fancy brass slot machine. On an impulse John shoved one of his pennies into the machine and pulled the handle. The cylinders spun with all their bright colored symbols, and as each cylinder stopped, a perfect score lined up. The magic door opened and an entire handful of pennies was disgorged from its entrails. John was astonished and enthralled. The amount was far more money than he had ever had in his life before. It bought great quantities of candy and led to many speculations about God.

Perhaps the church people were wrong in their assertion that the Scriptures were the word of God. Perhaps God was not a flinty being who punished children and resided in dark catacombs. Maybe God made and endorsed the lovely day and had awarded John luck as part of His blessing. Maybe God had a sense of humor even. Wouldn't that be interesting.

By 1927 John was being given more freedom than he had had in the past. If there was an idyllic time in his life, it was then, but even as it was happening, it was also being foreclosed. But of course he was not aware of that. Things were not going well for his father at all. Dan was falling more and more under the influence of alcohol, and he had abandoned almost all work at the Macdonalds' farm, while brother Dave was kept working almost like a personal slave, hired out to do gardening. Dave's small salary was extracted from him and kept by his father. Sales at the farm plummeted. Bill payments were ignored, and there was a languid inability in Dan to focus on business. He began to talk about moving away from his problems. Dan had been living in Montague probably longer than he had lived in any other community. From impressions he derived from reading Western literature, Dan spoke enthusiastically of the West, where he imagined there was more freedom and opportunity.

Dan's instability, alcoholism, and loud polemics about bills, mortgage payments, lawyers and bank managers, all distressed John who at the time was also undergoing sibling rivalry between himself and his brother Ron, two years his senior. But despite the stressed human relations, John and his brothers and sister managed to find niches in their lives into which they could fit many of the joys of childhood. The three boys were allowed to join the Boy Scouts. The association with other boys provided a forum for pleasant games, activities, and hiking. Mr. Trowbridge, the scout master, was a calm, placid man who allowed the boys a great range of freedom with very little attention to scouting curriculum. Also intermingled with the children's repression and emotional distress, the Macdonald children enjoyed the superb benefits of living in an ideal small town with all of its social activities of winter sports, hunting, fishing, boating, lake swimming, and above all the lush natural environment before it was degraded by the rubble of industry.

The boys found a beautiful designed dory that was wrecked, repaired and converted it into a sailboat, and they spent many happy hours sailing on White Lake. A short distance up the mouth of White River, which emptied into the lake, was a place called "the Booms," where in years past, timber floated down the river and was held in booms while waiting to be milled into lumber. It became the town boys' private nude swimming hole.

One of the greatest frolics of the year in a small village is Halloween, and the Macdonald boys enjoyed full participation in the evening activities. On Halloween evening, gangs of village boys gathered at dusk to rove through the village, writing with soap on people's windows, raiding private parties, looking for outdoor toilets to tip over, or a wagon to hoist onto the roof of someone's barn, or whatever other activity struck them as humorous. There was a resident by the name of Mr. Titus, a sedentary and extraordinarily fat man who always sat in his toilet the whole of

Halloween evening to anchor it down. His determination to protect his domain focused the attention of the boys and they tipped his toilet over anyway, with him in it. The outhouse landed with the door side down, so Mr. Titus was trapped. The distressed man had to tear the commode seat off and hoist his rotund self out through the opening. He probably did not think it was funny, but the boys thought it was hilarious.

One year the boys removed a world war cannon from the school yard, rolled it half a mile away, and dumped it down a gully just to enjoy watching it tumble through space. The following day the school principal called a general assembly meeting and told the kids he wasn't going to ask who the guilty persons were, but he would expect each guilty boy to take the rope, which he provided, march to the gully, and retrieve the cannon. Needless to say, every boy in the school turned out to bring the cannon back.

In spite of the excellent social advantages of the little village of Montague, the Macdonald family was tense with problems. The family tensions struck different members in different ways, depending upon the psyches on which they impinged. Brother Ron reacted with anger, frustration, and overt acts of aggression, while John became obsequious, shy, and indwelling. Ron often took his anger out on John, who was less muscular than his brother. John dreaded to come home from school because he knew that as soon as he got within range of Ron, he was going to be struck hard on the back with an open palm that would knock the wind out of him. The gesture was ostensibly an act of back-patting approval. Ron was oblivious to the pain he was causing.

On the other hand, if any other kid picked on John, Ron would fiercely rush to his brother's defense. John never quite knew where he stood with his brother Ron— was he hated or loved by him, or was it both? One thing was clear to John: Ron regarded his younger brother as being rather stupid. Ron enjoyed playing games with John and invariably Ron won because he had a much sharper mind for games. John indeed became convinced, that compared to his brother Ron, he was indeed stupid, so he shrank from playing the games that he could never win.

Brother Ron's more aggressive and rebellious nature was a source of irritation to his father, who undoubtedly contrasted it with the pliant behavior of his daughter and other two sons.

Dan often reacted to Ron with outburst of anger and verbal punishment, to which Ron reacted with bitter hostility. Dan would assign work for the kids to do on the farm, then leave to visit with his friends. Ron would rebel and run off to the local golf course to caddy for wealthy patrons who tipped him generously and kept him in spending money that he could never get at home. At last the situation became intolerable to Ron, and he ran away from home. He was away about a week before he returned. He never divulged where he had gone or how he had managed to survive, probably sleeping outdoors without a shelter. After Ron returned, Dan eased his disciplinary pressure and there developed a somewhat estranged tolerance for each other, a coexisting cease-fire in which neither challenged the other.

By 1927 Macdonald's farm was in bad shape. Dan had all but abandoned it, and the children could not carry on the business by themselves, even though they tried. The farm income was almost nil, and the greenhouse was run down from neglect. Sister Helen had grown discouraged with the situation and hired out to a wealthy couple who took her to live with them in Florida, to work as their maid. Family unity was in a state of disarray. Dan kept talking more and more about leaving Montague and going West. He hoped to leave all of his problems behind and start a new life in some Western state where he envisioned a future of warm climate, freedom, and who knows, even prosperity.

8

In the summer of 1927, a striking event took place that had unforeseen consequences for the Macdonald family. There was an unpaved road that led past the Macdonald farm, which extended out through scrub oak woods to a few remote scattered farmhouses. The road was rarely traveled except by an occasional exploratory driver. But during that summer, the back country road that led nowhere began to suddenly support an endless parade of cars going back and forth, raising great quantities of dust. It was all very mysterious to John. What possible reason could all those people have for driving out that country lane to nowhere?

One day in mid-summer, John was astonished to see five carloads of heavily armed police officers drive by the Macdonald farm at a high rate of speed on the rural country road, headed toward the abandoned farm houses. Later in the day, the police cars returned and all other traffic ceased. Out of curiosity John and his brothers hiked out to the farm houses to see if they could find out what went on there. From the distance of a quarter of a mile, a strong fermented odor made it suddenly clear what had happened. The farm house had been converted into a bootleg liquor distillery and sales office. The making and sale of alcoholic beverages was of course forbidden by the Eighteenth Amendment National Prohibition Act, in force at that time, so the police had raided the place and had used axes to chop open countless barrels of fermenting mash, which had all drained into the basement to form a pool a couple of feet deep. There was broken crockery and bottles everywhere.

The distilling retort had been removed from the premises for evidence in the oncoming trial, and only a few pieces of furniture and three radios remained intact in the house.

Now in 1927 a house with a radio in it was not very common. The broadcast business was just getting underway then. To find three radios all in one house was indeed exceptional. They were modern Atwater Kent sets, but very primitive by today's standards, with vacuum tubes and big variable tuning condensers, and even loudspeakers when most radios at that time had only ear phones for listening. Tuning to a station involved adjusting three tuning dials till one heard a high-frequency squealing whistle. As you got closer to adjustment for the broadcast station, the whistle decreased in frequency to a low growl till finally, with great satisfaction, the listener heard voices from afar.

John and his brothers left everything as it was and vacated the farm house, a little awed by the turn of events. A few days after the police raid, the three radios mysteriously appeared again, this time in the living room of the Macdonalds' house. It seemed that Dan had picked them up and brought them to the house at the request of the bootlegger, who Dan said had asked him to take care of them. Dan was of course fully knowledgeable about the raid and the contents of the farm house, for he had been spending much of his time there for the past months.

Brother Dave was directed to hook the best radio up to appropriate batteries and to construct an antenna atop the house, and the family evenings were soon enchanted by comedians Amos and Andy, and the tinny sounds of the Chicago Barn Dance. The connection to the world through radio was a very exciting event in John's life. From two hundred miles away from Chicago, you could hear the sharp smack of a baseball bat at Wrigley Field, the Cubs stadium, and the call of the umpire. What could be more exciting than that?

Nineteen twenty-seven was a vintage year for America. Technology was swelling to a swagger, radios, refrigerators, cars, airplanes, ocean liners—all of it generating such an aura of self-confident optimism that the financial markets were booming as never before in the history of the nation. Al Capone was reputed to have made a hundred million dollars in illicit liquor trade, Charles Lindbergh flew nonstop over the Atlantic to Europe and was hailed as an American icon, Babe Ruth swatted his sixtieth home run, the last Model-T Ford car was built amid preparations for the new refined Model A, and there was a feeding frenzy of stock investments that produced reams of paper wealth. But buried beneath the pyramids of ticker tape were dark economic tombs invisible to most investors and ignored by others who should have known better.

One morning several weeks after the bistro bust of the bootleg house, the Macdonald residence phone rang.

"Is this W 650?" the caller asked. "Yes," Dan answered. The message that followed visibly shook him. Dan quickly called Dave and told him to disconnect the living room radio they were using and hide all three radios in the shop, a shanty building attached to the chicken house. No sooner had the three radios been hidden away than a car load of police drove in with a search warrant. In short order they found the radios and confiscated them. Dan was taken into custody for possessing stolen property and incarcerated in the Muskegon County jail. Two days went by before Dan arranged bail and came home much subdued. He claimed that he had been set up by the bootlegger and that he was innocently keeping the radios till the man could retrieve them. It was a thin alibi that no one accepted. But during those two days, Dan had made a decision to take his family and leave the woes of Montague for the wilds of the West, and a new life. He had been thinking about making just such a move for a long time and his impulse was now impelled to action by the turn of events.

Like many Midwest and Eastern people, at that time, Dan was influenced by the popular authors who wrote about the West, such as Bret Harte and Zane Grey, and by the advent of popular Western movies; highly fantasized stories set in the imaginary free-spirited Eden of open land sparsely populated by rugged Western frontiersmen. The Western cult, as simple and unreal as it was, generated a special mind set among Eastern people that promoted the quest for a Western grail on the Pacific side of the continent.

Dan's tendency to speculate in adventurous propositions dovetailed with his romanticized Western fantasies. Dan had only a third grade education, other than his education of practical experience, and so his knowledge of geography was deplorable. He had no idea of where he wished to go in the West, only a vague notion that he wanted to move in that direction. Sometimes in an alcoholic haze he would mumble unintelligibly about going West through the Floridas and the Georgias. Anyone attempting to point out that there wasn't any such route would be summarily dismissed. The idea of the venture was more important than the details of getting there. For sure, years of cold Michigan and Wisconsin winters added to the attractiveness of a warmer climate, perhaps in the Southwest where he could start a new life, and so he started to organize a family agenda toward that goal.

By selling household items, Dan managed to scrape together two hundred dollars to finance the trip West. To insure that the bank didn't discover his hidden assets and confiscate them pursuant to the mortgage foreclosure, he and Mary hid the money in a mason jar and stealthily buried it, at night, in the family garden plot, to await the time for moving. The old Nash touring car was traded in for a more modern 1926 Nash sedan, with the luxury of roll-up windows and a fabric covered hard top, a self-starter instead of the hand-engine crank (as in the old car), and most innovative for the time, four wheel brakes.

While trying the new car out, Dan applied the brakes hard to see how reliable four-wheel brakes really were. There was such an unexpected abrupt stop that he was thrown violently forward and the tires screeched. Dan angrily announced that brakes stopping a car that fast were dangerous, so he disconnected the front brakes permanently, muttering about stupid ideas.

The Nash engine was not in the best of shape, so Dan cast about for an auto mechanic to repair it at home for a reasonable price. The person he selected was a nephew of Mary's named Cash Thompson. Cash assured Dan that he would put the Nash in guaranteed top condition for thirty dollars. Thirty dollars in 1928, to an unemployed auto mechanic, was an excellent deal. Cash went to work with vigor and enthusiasm. But evidently, Cash the auto mechanic, was not quite as good at his work as he proclaimed. The overhaul of the Nash engine went on for weeks. Perhaps there may have been an ulterior motive for the slow progress, for he was also getting free board and meals at the Macdonald house. But even after he finished the job, there was some malfunction and the whole engine had to be stripped down and done over. However, Dan never lost faith, and also he had found that Cash, the auto mechanic, was an amiable person to imbibe with during the long overhaul job.

During the time the car was being overhauled, Brother Dave was directed to take the old Model-T Ford delivery truck, which had been formerly used on the Macdonald farm, and hack-saw the frame in half just behind the driver's seat, so that the truck bed, rear axle, and wheels were left intact on the rear half of the frame. A trailer hitch was bolted to this remaining truck bed assembly, and a neat canopy top erected over the truck bed to form one of the first generation travel trailers.

During this period of planning and activity to prepare for the move West, the greenhouse was abandoned and left unheated during the cold autumn weather. Thousands of plants froze or dried up for lack of water. All the chickens from the chicken house were slaughtered and the meat canned for future food en route. Topsy, the crumpled horned family cow, was sold, and for John that was an upsetting day. Topsy had a sentimental value rooted in the practicality of her rich milk, and also the animal warmth of her welcomed droppings on cold frosty mornings to defrost the boy's bare feet, and then there was her seemingly good sense of humor when she learned which apple tree branches she could run under to wipe riders off of her back. John was saddened to see such a good friend leave.

A loosely planned undetailed itinerary was forming in Dan's mind for the trip West. Mary had a remote relative who had migrated West years before and had homesteaded a farm somewhere near Medford, Oregon.

The owner had died and the land was left unclaimed by relatives. Because of delinquent taxes, the title had reverted back to the county. Dan had some vague notion of finding the place, paying up the taxes, and claiming it. Dan had a friend and ex-neighbor, John Bedoe, who had moved to Oregon from Montague a number of years previously. Dan wrote to Bedoe and asked about the opportunity for work in Oregon. Bedoe wrote back with an impressive report about the area, but warned that jobs were hard to find.

The 1928 Christmas season was approaching, but there was little reason for holiday cheer at the Macdonald farm. Always prior to this, the boys had prepared for the holiday by venturing out into the local woods to cut a Christmas tree. It was set up in the parlor and decorated with fragile glass balls and strings of tinsel. It was before the time of Christmas tree lights. Generally the kids got gifts of new underwear and socks, practical things—no toys. But this year there was no tree and no preparation for a family gathering. Ostensibly there were no gifts either, but secretly Brother Dave had been making a pair of snow skis for John. On Christmas day he gave them to him. John was amazed and overwhelmed by this most beautiful gift from his older brother. Dave had probably spent months crafting them for John's height and size—he was eleven years old then. The skis were handsomely decorated in bright red pin stripping and varnished to a brilliant gloss.

The sheer joy of the gift was so great that John was overcome by it, and he embarrassed his brother by crying with tears of happiness. Never had he been given such a wonderful gift in his entire life. Unfortunately the Michigan winter was late in coming that year, so there was no snow on the ground to try the skis out. Therefore the skis were lovingly left leaning against the side of the barn to await the first snow.

After Christmas the household furniture was gathered up: kitchen table and chairs, the living-room buffet and Morris rocker, the foot treadle sewing machine, the victrola phonograph and records, the pump organ, the pots and pans and dishes, the lovely pure silver family tea set that had never been used, and all the acquisitions from years of family life; all were transported to the home of an aunt of Mary's and stored in her barn.

Then began the packing away of all those things into the trailer that the family would take West with them: canned food, clothing, a few pots and pans and dishes, bedding; practical tools like shovels, ax, saws, and carpenter tools. This was not like an ordinary trip, but rather it was an expedition into a new life. Over the top of the trailer load was erected a double-bunk bed, and thus the trailer became a more or less self-contained unit to live out of during the trip and even afterward in the vague destination of Oregon.

On New Year's Day 1929, Dan hooked up the trailer to the Nash car, loaded his three sons and the family white collie dog, Spot, into the back seat, with he and Mary in front, and drove away from the family farm and home that had served them for the past twelve years. It was a bitterly cold day, with a threatening snowstorm about to sweep in off Lake Michigan. John looked back at the old clapboard house that had sheltered him in his childhood, the site of so many painful experiences rooted in the cruelty of his stepmother, but there had been wonderful times too: the joy of children's friendship and kind neighbors, the verdant farm lands and woods in which the children could wander and dream the dreams of childhood, and there was the pristine lake and beaches and all the accompanying aquatic adventures of boating, fishing, ice skating, and there were his grammar school chums and the teachers, all of it slipping by the car and receding into the past as they sped out of Montague, heading west.

As they drove away, John looked back one last time, and there resting against the side of the barn was the beautiful pair of skis that brother Dave had made for him that

Christmas. John had never once had the opportunity to use them. Quickly the greatest gift of his childhood slipped away out of sight in a blur of tears. In a few moments they were out of town and on their way West and the book of John's childhood turned a page, and all of it passed into the shadows of the recesses of his mind.

The year of 1929 was the beginning of the longest and deepest economic depression in American history, and it had perhaps a more profound effect on its citizens than all the wars, hardships, and events that preceded it. It changed the optimism and bright hope that had previously always existed, even in the worst of times, to a shattering doubt about a sustainable future. People who lived through it were forever gripped by the fear of its return, and yet they also exulted in having been forged and tempered by its hardship.

The Macdonald farm had failed. The bank had foreclosed the mortgage and Dan and his family, except Helen who had left home, were beginning their westward migration along with thousands of other Americans who would soon follow from the Midwest, the South, the East in the second great migration to the Western side of the continent, the first mass migration having occurred in the Gold Rush and pioneering years.

Actually the beginning of their trip was southward down the Lake Michigan easterly coast line toward the Indiana border. They had started out and were driving into the teeth of a biting winter snowstorm, which began to accumulate large drifts on the highway. Pulling the trailer through the fresh snow labored the Nash engine, but not unduly, yet by the time they reached the Indiana border, the engine began to develop a sharp knock that rapidly deteriorated into a complete breakdown. They were just across the border on the outskirts of the city of South Bend.

Dan managed to pull off to the side of the highway in front of a little residential cottage, and there the family remained while the storm gathered its full force. The car was soon covered with snow. Dan asked the people, whose house they had stalled in front of, to use their phone to call a tow truck, but without success because it was New Year's Day and no garages were open. It was about four o'clock in the afternoon. Depressed, Dan returned to the car and announced that the family would have to make do and remain there till the following day.

The boys and the dog all huddled together in the back seat, and Dan and Mary bundled together in the front seat while snow drifted down over the car throughout the night. It was miserably cold and cramped. During the night Dan must have reviewed in his mind the competence of Cash, the auto mechanic, who had finished overhauling the car engine only the week before. When morning came at last, the good people in front of whose house they had broken down, kindly brought Dan and Mary a hot steaming cup of coffee, but they completely ignored the children, who were equally cold and hungry.

Dan telephoned for a tow truck to pull the car and trailer into a local garage in South Bend, where an assessment was made of the damaged engine. It was found that a crankshaft bearing had failed, but also all the bearings had been fitted so sloppily that they all had to be replaced. In those days, crankshaft bearings had to be hand-cast and hand-scraped to fit the crankshaft.

It would be about two full days' work to put the car engine into working order again.

The garage building was an enormous open edifice with an old pot-bellied stove at one side of the room, and next to the stove was a pile of broken hard rubber battery cases that were used for fuel in the heating stove. Burning the battery cases gave off such copious amounts of heat that the whole stove glowed cherry red like a blast furnace, but across the neighborhood drifted vast amounts of jet black sooty smoke that settled on the fresh snow turning it from white to black. A ragtag group of unemployed men, dressed in patched bib overalls, were gathered around the hot stove from morning to night, playing game after game of checkers to pass the time away while the blizzard raged outside. It was an interesting two days' wait for the car repair, especially for brother Ron, who was something of an expert at checkers, and spent his time winning nickel and dime bets. But if Ron came out ahead, the cost of the repairs to Dan must have cut drastically into his meager funds that he had collected to finance his trip West.

After getting on the road again, they drove southward through Indiana, and then southwestward toward the Mississippi River, where Dan studied the maps intently to find a bridge where he would not have to pay a toll charge to cross. They soon found that the storm, which had followed their departure from Michigan, had dumped such torrential rains in the South that cities and highways were flooded everywhere.

John had never been outside of his home state of Michigan before except for a brief stay one summer in Chicago, Illinois, so he was unprepared for the appalling sight of the impoverished shacks that the Southern black people lived in. Somewhere in Arkansas they found an unflooded village in which to make an overnight stop. Throughout the little town, John was impressed by the great number of pecan trees lining the streets, with great quantities of nuts on the ground. The boys enthusiastically gathered pecans and ate them to supplement their limited food supply.

After their overnight rest stop, Dan continued on his southwesterly route to avoid the winter snow to the north. They made it into northern Texas, where another disaster struck them. While crossing over a railroad track, the car bounced and the trailer hitch broke. They limped into a little village blacksmith shop where Dan bargained for it to be welded for five dollars. There was a feeling of redneck hostility among the local people that was palpable to the senses. Depression poverty was settling in and causing a sullen resentment that was readily directed against strangers. When the repair was finished, Dan paid for it with a twenty dollar bill. The blacksmith refused to give him back his fifteen dollars change. Dan was furious and a sharp argument ensued. Reluctantly, after Dan threatened to call the police, the change was handed over and the family was on their way again, relieved to be gone from the hostile atmosphere.

The next day they made it into New Mexico on the historically famous Route 66, the highway over which there would be an endless cavalcade in the next few years of thousands of impoverished families grasping desperately to find a better life than that of the failing Dust Belt farms of the Southeast, or the depression-failed businesses and factories of the Midwest and Eastern states, most of the people heading for California in hopeful expectation of a better new life.

At last the deplorable shacks of the Southern black people and the poor tenant farmers were behind them. Now they were beginning to see the neat pink-and-white stucco houses of New Mexico and Arizona. Dan found a place to camp on the outskirts of a small Arizona town. There the family stayed for a day of rest near a tourist motel, except that it was long before the term "motel" was invented—they were called auto cottages. The Macdonalds observed the motel's luxuriant flower garden that was blooming in midwinter when Michigan would be covered with snow. The contrast was novel. Dan, assuming the same winter gardens would be found in Oregon, was charged with optimism. But there was one small problem: he was now out of money to continue the trip West.

Without excessive stress over their financial circumstances, for Dan was never at a loss for some kind of resourcefulness, he sent a telegram to John's Uncle Elmer, the husband of Dan's wife's sister, who lived in Muskegon, Michigan, asking to borrow fifty dollars from him to continue the trip.

The money was promptly telegraphed back to Arizona, probably at the cost of privation, for they were poor people too. Now all the funds that Dan had accumulated for the trip being exhausted, all he could do was borrow from whomever he could to continue the Oregon odyssey, and none could be paid back during the depression. If he worried about it, it did not show; outwardly he seemed little concerned. In general people kept believing the economy would soon turn around and all would be well—Dan among them. Instead the recession plunged on downward to a depression and seemingly endless years would go by before there was returning hope.

Back on the road again, financed by relatives, they began the steep climb into the Hualapoi Mountains, heading toward the Colorado River and the border of California. The Macdonalds were inveterate flat-landers who had no previous experience or exposure to mountains before and were astonished at their grandeur. The depths of the awesome roadside cliffs and the steep inclines of the mountain highway were frightening.

The Nash touring car, pulling its trailer, began to falter and overheat. Auto engines of that period were equipped with a fuel delivery device called a "vacuum tank" that siphoned gasoline from the gas tank up to the engine to deliver it to the carburetor. It was before the use of fuel pumps. Unfortunately at high altitudes, the fuel would boil and vaporize in the vacuum tank and that broke the vacuum. Then the carburetor, starved for fuel, ceased functioning and the engine stalled—often in the middle of the highway.

It was then necessary to crawl under the car and open a little drain valve in the gas tank, draw out a pint or so of fuel, and pour it into the top of the vacuum tank, restart the engine and continue up-grade while the whole cycle repeated itself.

After quite a number of these failures, it began to look like the old Nash car would not be able to get the family over the mountains and into California. But about that time a huge cattle truck came slowly grinding up the grade in compound gear. Dan hailed the driver and he stopped. They bargained together to hook the Nash on behind the truck and be pulled to the top. A price for towing was set at one dollar and that was how they got over the last hurdle en route to California. Brother Dave was steering the Nash, and from time to time, he would use the car engine to help the trucker. This started a violent argument with Dan shouting, "Don't do that. It uses our gasoline. I paid him a whole dollar to tow us." At that time one dollar would buy about seven gallons of gasoline at about fifteen cents per gallon.

After the tow to the top of the mountain pass, they were free to start down the western side of the grade. The whole family was relieved of worry and everyone relaxed as they wound their way down to the Colorado River. There they stopped to stretch their legs and gaze at the scenery. The family dog was let out to exercise, and when they got back into the car to drive on, no one noticed that the dog was missing.

Only after driving perhaps twenty miles was it noticed that Spot was not in the car. A debate ensued as to whether to go back for the dog and consume more precious gasoline, or abandon her and go on. There was a unanimous decision to return to the river, and there she was found almost exactly where she had been let out of the car, waiting patiently with complete confidence to be picked up.

That day's journey brought them past the town of Needles and over the California border. From the Arizona mountain heights, the family had looked down into the California panorama before them, verdant farm lands and date palms in the distance—such a welcome sight after the trauma of snowstorms, engine failure, breakdowns, and the awesome challenge of the Arizona mountains. Dave and Ron crawled into the trailer to sleep and John fell asleep in the back seat of the car while Dan drove on toward the California desert. Very shortly they were brought to a stop again, this time by the California border guard. Dan was surprised that there was such a thing as a border guard. No other state that they had been through had their borders guarded. A little chagrined by the event, Dan made some disparaging remarks about California and of course the guardsmen bristled back, demanding to know how much money Dan had. It seemed that California, attempting to discourage the depression-impoverished people who were pouring into the sunny habitat, had passed a law that before outsiders could move into California, they now had to have funds to support themselves.

Dan was incensed, and it may be noted that the law was shortly after that declared unconstitutional.

The guards also demanded to inspect the trailer. Dan lifted the rear trailer curtain and the guardsmen were startled to find four bare feet protruding out the rear. Shocked as they were, they obviously were thinking they had stumbled onto two corpses being transported into California. Dan, much amused, explained that it was his two sons in there and routed them out to show they were alive. As for the support funds, Dan explained that his destination was Oregon, so the guards waved him on.

The drive across the Mohave Desert was the next stage of their trip West and was another shock to the Macdonald family. Never had they seen such a hostile barren wasteland of sand and cactus plants. This was California! Where were the fruit orchards, the vineyards? Where were the orange groves? The family gazed out upon mile after mile of parched landscape that they were passing through and could not help but contrast it with the neat farms and green pastures, and the lush Michigan woods that they had left behind. The vast open sweep of the desert was unsettling like crossing an ocean, and they felt vulnerable.

Aroused by curiosity, Dan stopped out in the middle of nowhere, just to observe the seemingly lifeless land. They discussed whether there was any creature that could live in this severe environment.

Everyone was feeling a curious sense of depression about California when Dan suddenly emitted a shriek of terror and began leaping about like a madman. John recalled reading of a Scottish dance called "The Highland Fling," and this expression came to mind as he looked on in astonishment at his father gyrating across the Mohave Desert and shrieking like he was crazy. Dan flicked his suspenders off and began pulling down his trousers even while jumping around. He kicked off his pants, and clad only in long underwear, he shook a desert lizard out of his trouser leg. None of them had ever seen one of these scaly reptiles before. Dan was sure it was poisonous, causing him to react with hysteria. The boys thought it was hilarious, but Dan didn't think it was funny at all. The incident did serve to prove that there was animal life on the desert.

After seemingly endless miles of open California desert, they made it into the central San Joaquin Valley and were happy to observe that California did have vast amounts of rich tillable land. They now turned northward toward the Oregon border. A day later they were in Eugene, Oregon, and the trip West was ended. Here the family was to begin a new life.

9

Eugene, Oregon, was a sparkling clean, neat community of about fifteen thousand people. The town had the feeling of stability about it that long-established Eastern towns had, notwithstanding that like everywhere in America at that time, they were undergoing an economic collapse.

Dan began immediately to search for a cheap house to rent. Without much effort, he found a clean two-bedroom house on a shady tree-lined residential street for twelve dollars a month, a bargain even at that time.

The boys set about exploring the premises and soon discovered a quart-size jar of peanut butter, probably several years old, that someone had left on a shelf. Always hungry and especially short rationed during the trip West, they quickly hid the jar under their clothing, retreated to the garage, whittled spoons from scraps of wood, and ate the whole jar all within a few minutes.

Dan's next step was to look up his old neighbor, John Bedoe, whom he had corresponded with, and who had moved to Oregon from Michigan many years before the Macdonalds arrived. Bedoe was probably not very enthusiastic when Dan and his whole family appeared unexpectedly on his doorstep in January of 1929, but he treated them kindly. With this mild accolade of a greeting, Dan was encouraged to ask for a loan of a hundred dollars. Probably, Dan in his mind, had already calculated he would have to settle for a lesser amount. They came to terms for sixty dollars.

John, at age eleven, was entered into Roosevelt Junior High School to continue his education, and brothers Dave and Ron explored the town and outlying area to occupy their time.

Oregon public schools, unlike Michigan, required students to buy their own textbooks and school supplies. But Dan was not persuaded to the idea of buying books. Probably he assumed that when John attended school for a while, the school would accede to his need and provide for the books somehow. But that never happened; he was left to flounder day after day with neither books nor school supplies. Students were also required to buy gym clothing and shoes, and so without proper clothing, he could not participate in gym activities either. Somehow Sister Helen, who was working for a barely sustainable salary as a maid in Florida, gathered enough money together to buy a school clothing outfit for him. Had it not been for her generosity, he could not have attended school at all.

John flubbed about trying to do school assignments without books for a month or more, but the problem was soon to be resolved by drastic means, for Dan suddenly yanked him out of school because he had found a job that the boys could all participate in. So at barely age twelve, John's public schooling ended abruptly to begin a work career, and he was never again given an opportunity to return to school even though the act was illegal at the time.

It had not occurred to John's father, nor did he ever understand that what he had done was a tragedy for his son. After all Dan had left school in the third grade and had begun working then, so why should be have any remorse for taking John out of school to start a work career in the seventh grade? By Dan's standards, John understood that he was fortunate to have been allowed even that much public education. Dan had taken both of John's brothers out of school at age fourteen. Sister Helen was the only one of the children who was allowed to finish high school, and she continued on for one year of college.

John was ever after to resent this abrupt interruption of his basic American right to a public school education, and he spent years and years afterward attempting to dispel the loss by acquiring self-education through reading, correspondence courses, and junior college studies. Unfortunately there is no way that later compensating education can make up for the socialization that is learned in the public school environment. Probably the learned social skills acquired in public schools are as important, if not more important, than the academic knowledge. Without the vital framework of school fraternity, John grew up to be at variance with others of his age and was endlessly plagued by inhibitions and a profound feeling of being outside the human race, viewing his fellow man as from a distance, and because of the added cruelty of his stepmother, he saw the human world always in a context of fear of it.

The job that Dan had found for the family was one of the government-sponsored projects that the state of Oregon was establishing to help people who were out of work and suffering deplorable economic difficulties. A large contracting firm, McNutt and Company, which built bridges and highways, obtained a contract to widen state Highway 38 along the Umqua River between Elkton and Reedsport, about twenty miles of roadway through virgin growth timber land. Individual families or small groups of workmen subcontracted with the prime contractor for a length of roadway in which to cut the trees down and clear all the brush a hundred feet from the side of the presently narrow highway. This was preliminary to the tractors and heavy equipment moving in to do the grading and paving. Dan contracted to do a one-thousand-foot stretch of roadway. He bought a tent for them to sleep in, gathered together a few cooking utensils and some tools, and set out with the old Nash car for the Umqua River with his three sons. Mary was left in Eugene, to live with the Bedoe family.

Neither Dan nor the boys had any experience in felling trees of the size they were about to undertake. Michigan trees were all dwarfs when compared with these monsters of virgin growth in almost a rain-forest climate. They also soon found out that their thousand-foot section of highway had the largest Douglas fir tree on it that could be found anywhere in the West—fully as large as any thousand-year-old redwood.

The Macdonald section of highway passed through a flood plain of very rich soil that supported a jungle growth of vine maple, rhododendrons, blackberry tangles, and poison oak, amongst giant trees of Port-Orford cedar, silver firs, and Douglas fir. Having been reared in Michigan, the entire entanglement of vines, shrubs, and trees was unidentifiable to the Macdonalds. Someone casually told them that the red-leafed vines were poison oak, but they paid little heed to the warning.

Across the river from their contract section was a large sheep ranch, to which there was no access road on that side of the stream. The ranch owner had therefore looped a cable across the river on pulleys, to which was tethered an auto ferry, and by which he could transport himself and his car back and forth to his ranch. It was a clever design in which the current of the river propelled the ferry barge. The rancher had built a garage on the Macdonald's side of the river to put his car in, in times of flood when it would be dangerous to cross on the ferry. The ranch owner kindly offered Dan the use of the garage to store tools and supplies in. It was just a shack of a building and infested with rats and not fit to use as living quarters. It was near the garage that Dan decided to pitch their tent and set up a campsite to work out of.

From the tool crib of the McNutt Company, Dan was issued two-man cross-cut saws, sledges and wedges, double-bitted axes, and brush hooks.

The family set to work with zeal. Dave and Ron felled the trees and cut them up into firewood, John cut brush and burned it, and Dan supervised, sharpened tools, and did the cooking, pleading that cooking was an especially hard job because he had to stay up all through the night to cook cornmeal for breakfast for the three boys. They knew of course that his special pleading was nonsense, that cornmeal can be cooked in about a half hour, but they never challenged his family authority. For John, barely age twelve and malnourished, the work was very hard, but he picked up woodsmen's skills and soon learned how to use tools effectively.

At first Dan teamed up with John on a two-man saw to cut up logs into firewood lengths. The saws were eight feet long and required a long swinging stroke to clear the sawdust. John soon learned that Dan had a tendency to pull the saw to one side on the return stroke, called "whipping," which doubled and tripled the required effort. Already exhausted from the hard work, the addition of a partner who whipped the saw to one side made it impossible to work with Dan. Worse yet, Dan was continually yelling at John that he wasn't working hard enough. The job soon became a living hell, and John broke down and begged to be allowed to work by himself. Dan, disgruntled, accepted the plea and returned to cooking cornmeal all night.

Much of the vines and undergrowth to be cut down and

burned was poison oak, to which the family paid no attention because they did not know what it would do to them.

Neither did they know that the smoke from burning poison oak, when ingested into their lungs, would cause internal poisoning, and daily they both physically contacted the poison oak and inhaled the smoke while burning it. Inevitably all of them acquired massive poisoning from both contact and the smoke.

At night they all slept in the tent together in a row of bodies, and John slept next to his father. The work was so hard that even with the severe itching rashes of poison oak, John fell into deep sleep. But the body seeks to adjust itself even during sleep, and one night John's nausea was so intense, that in spite of being asleep, he turned over and vomited straight into his father's face. Dan had a long bristly mustache that absorbed much of the discharge from which it dripped down over his mouth and chin. Dan leaped out of bed, cussing John, and rushed down to the river to clean himself up.

Upon returning he yelled at John, "I will never sleep beside you again!"

With that outburst he snatched up his blanket and moved into the shack of a garage to sleep among the rats. But that night's problems were not over for him. Because of the rats, he slept fully clothed and next morning pointed out to the boys multiple rat tracks across his clothing. It seemed that the rats had discovered their supply of flour, and all through the night they kept running across Dan, leaving a trail of floured rat tracks. Dan refused to return to the tent to sleep at night, but to ward off the garage rats, he acquired a number of rat traps and set them throughout the shed.

Then from a trash dump Dan found an old car axle weighing about ten pounds, this to use as a shillelagh to bludgeon the creatures. During the middle of the night, after that, the boys were much amused to first hear the snap-snap of the rat traps springing closed and then a terrible commotion of rats being beaten with the car axle, after which the garage door would be flung open, and in a shaft of lamp light, a number of rats flung out the door. Following the event there would be peace and quiet for an hour followed by repeated episodes throughout the night, and then from time to time, Dan would get up and stir his corn meal, which was cooking on a camp stove, and which he insisted had to be cooked all night. The number of rats seemed inexhaustible during the following weeks, but Dan's passion for the job was also inexhaustible, and there developed a rat war in which each morning Dan would announce how many trapped rats he had beat with his car axle during the night.

The Umpqua semi-rainforest climate was habitat for a great number of interesting animals, the most prominent of which was a creature about the size of a small cat that local people called a mountain boomer. The name was undoubtedly a variation of the more commonly heard name, mountain beaver or "Sewellel." He was a little brown stub-tailed fellow with a teddy bear friendly face, and he seemed completely without fear of people. He would often sit a few feet away on a stump, looking poised and amused watching the boys work. His presence was very entertaining.

The local sheep ranches were often plagued by coyotes and mountain lions, and an occasional black bear that would get in the habit of killing lambs. The rancher, across the river from the Macdonald's encampment, kept two enormous bloodhounds that were specially trained to track bears. The red droop-eared dogs, Jake and Jacob, with such sad loose-skinned faces that the weight of the world seemed to be borne by their expressions, were famous throughout the county. Whenever a bear was found to be killing a rancher's lambs, Jake and Jacob's services would be telephoned for to track the predator till he was brought to quarry and shot. Once the dogs had picked up the scent, they would pursue day and night till they intercepted him. They were taught not to attack but merely hold the animal at bay, for the bear could easily kill the dogs in a battle. They would stay just outside of the range of the bear's fierce claws and sound their "bear at bay" song till the hunter could get there and shoot the animal. Sometimes the hunt would carry on for days and the hunter would become exhausted, give up, and go home, but Jake and Jacob, far out ahead on the trail, would continue their dogged pursuit by themselves.

The Macdonalds were warned that the dogs might carry on the hunt for days till they too became exhausted, at which time they would eventually return to the river garage where Dan was sleeping at night. The rancher would then pick them up from there and take them back across the river and home.

Sure enough, one night after the dogs had been out on a hunt for days, Jake and Jacob dashed into the boys' tent late in the night, emaciated, thirsty, and hungry, tongues lolling out and panting, but overjoyed in their greeting, slurping everyone's faces with their tails thumping an enthusiastic greeting, and looking ever so sad. They had done their best, but bruin had gotten away from them. The boys fed and gave the dogs water, and opened the garage door where Dan was sleeping. Jake and Jacob happily entered and curled up beside Dan for a well-earned sleep, perhaps to dream about the bear they had been tracking and that had got away into the next county.

At last it became time to cut down the enormous Douglas fir tree that was on the Macdonald's section of highway. The tree was known to everyone in the area and was looked upon as a sort of landmark monument. Dave and Ron examined it carefully to try to determine how it could be felled so it would not block the road for traffic. To complicate matters, the butt of the tree had been repeatedly burned by forest fires to form a deep hollow in the trunk, making it very difficult to determine just which way it would fall when it was cut. In spite of its burned trunk, the tree was basically healthy and the boys could see it was going to be a challenge to fall the monster.

From the McNutt tool crib, they checked out the longest cross-cut saw available, a twelve-footer and clearly inadequate for the job.

However, since the butt of the tree was burned so deeply, it made it possible for one man to stand within the hollowed section, to work the saw, while his partner, on the other end of the saw, worked from the perimeter of the tree. This was a very dangerous way to fell a tree, but there was no alternative with the tools they had to work with. The person working within the hollowed-out section would have to get out of there well before the tree came down. Since Ron was only fourteen years old and therefore smaller-bodied than Dave, it fell to him to work inside of the hollow. John worried for his brother throughout the cutting operation.

They started the job in the morning and endless time seemed to pass before the saw cut was deep enough to weaken the tree at about one o'clock in the afternoon. All the highway traffic had to be stopped well before the tree was about to fall for fear that it might fall on a passing car. This meant that the highway had to be closed for a couple of hours waiting for the massive tree to come down. Brother Ron got out of the hollowed trunk well before the tree was weakened enough to fall, but because the two-man saw was not long enough to cut straight through the trunk, they then had to cut diagonally across each corner of the main kerf to weaken the tree further, but also making it harder to determine just where it would fall. Although the intention was to fall the tree parallel to the highway, when it finally crashed, the hollow section of the tree caused it to pivot as it went down and it fell angling across the highway.

It then became necessary to immediately cut a section of the trunk out that would be wide enough to let cars pass through. Those two cuts to remove a gigantic log out of the way of the traffic took well over another hour of extremely hard work with saws that were far too short for the job. At last the contractor sent in a bulldozer tractor and pushed the log free of the road to open the highway some three hours after the traffic had first been stopped.

John took a tape measurement of this first cut and found that the tree was thirteen feet in diameter at this point, which was about twenty feet up the trunk of the tree. At ground level the Douglas fir must have been over sixteen feet in diameter. It was difficult to get an accurate measurement of the base because of the deeply hollowed trunk.

A brief discussion took place about what to do with a thirteen-foot diameter log, and then without hesitation, the bulldozer driver shoved it down the river bank into the Umqua to float out to sea. That one log probably would have produced enough clear lumber, without a single knot, to build an entire house. The whole tree was then summarily cut up into logs and disposed of in the Umqua River to float to the ocean and waste. No one gave it a second thought; such was the prodigal waste in that time of history.

There was a sadness about this event that grew ever greater with the years, as John recalled it, when he became more acutely aware that he had participated in destroying a part of Oregon's heritage. It was done so thoughtlessly, so carelessly, on everyone's part from the local people who did not value the magnificent tree, to the contractor who thought of it as merely a nuisance, to an engineering draftsman in some distant office who drew a straight line on a blueprint where the highway was to be built when he could have as easily drawn a line around it. The event might be described in the biblical term "Original Sin," a day in 1929 when a bit of Oregon's Eden was lost. Now as cars hurtle by over that section of highway, the drivers will never know that on that spot stood perhaps the largest, most magnificent Douglas fir tree that Oregon ever produced, and it was just thoughtlessly cut down and pushed into the Umqua River to float out to sea.*

One day while the boys were working on the Umqua River job, a battered old car pulled up and stopped, and an old gentleman stepped out. He asked if he could examine a certain tree that they were about to cut down and burn. It was a small tree, perhaps eight inches in diameter, with deep green leaves that had a strong aromatic odor when they were crushed. On the side of the tree was an enormous tumorlike growth about three feet in diameter. The man explained that it was a myrtle tree burl, and that Oregon myrtle was a valuable hardwood used in making all sorts of wooden artifacts because of its golden hue coloration and ability to take a high polish. If the burl proved to be solid inside, he would buy it for five dollars. Five dollars was a

---

*This story about the Douglas fir tree, in edited form, was first published in the 100th edition of *Fine Wood Working* magazine, by the Taunton Press in 1993, with the proviso that Taunton Press must be notified if the story ever is to be republished, and that republishing it must be accompanied by a written footnote that *Fine Wood Working* magazine was the original publisher.

good day's wages then, so they eagerly sold it to him to make veneer out of it.

It was from such events, as the value of the myrtle tree burl, that John began to acquire a lifelong love affair with wood and woodworking that was to sustain his spirit through many a dark hour in his later life. The Umqua River job was an enriching experience, but weighed against the sacrifice of a full public school education, he felt he had suffered a loss that would never be recovered.

When the job was finished, the McNutt Company already had obtained another contract near Crater Lake, of a different sort. A severe fire had whipped through a dense forest area bordering a secondary county road at a place called "Walk and Push Hill."

Their job was to strip off the burned bark on the still-living trees, chop down the fire-burned shrubs and dead trees, blast out the stumps, level the blasting craters, and return the land to a parklike environment. Dan bid for a section to work on and his bid was accepted. So he and the boys packed their camp gear and tools into the old Nash car, and moved on to "Walk and Push Hill." It proved to be suitably named.

At no time did Dan ever tell the boys how much money they had made at the Umqua job. Whatever amount it was, he took possession of it and never offered the boys so much as pocket change, notwithstanding the fact that they had done almost all of the work. Yet in defense of Dan's attitude, it was completely in keeping with the standards of his youth, in which the father of a family had absolute dictatorial control over all members. Dan would have been loath to think of his actions as selfish or like slavery, yet his sons were indeed like personal slaves.

It was a lifestyle that was not very different from what occurred in countless other nineteenth- and early twentieth-century American families. As head of the family, the father's role was to direct the work of his sons, provide the supplies and tools, be the boss and collect and disperse profits. It would never have occurred to the boys to challenge this chattel system in which they could be used by their father to whatever ends pleased him. They grumbled but they never rebelled. They had been trained to be as obedient as draft animals, and they submitted to such strictures as by Pavlovian conditioning. Their rancor only generated self-guilt.

Dan had probably been subjected to this same ironbound discipline in his childhood, so he was unconsciously just carrying on what he regarded as the traditional role of a rural American father.

The "Walk and Push Hill" job was located in a stately stand of ponderosa pine, with an undergrowth of tough yew wood and brambles, and the ever-present poison oak. All of it had scorched just enough to fire harden the brush. Dan equipped brothers Dave and Ron with climbing spurs with suspension ropes looped about their waists, and set them to work climbing trees, often to a height of sixty feet or more, where with a hand axe they were to peel off the burnt black outside tree bark, leaving intact the inner bark to make the trees look nice again. It was a dangerous job; one wrong swing of the razor sharp axe could cut their own safety rope. Quantities of black powdery char rained down upon them as they worked, and when they came down from the trees, their entire bodies were as black as coal miners.

Standing trees that had been killed by the fire were to be felled, the limbs trimmed, and the trunks cut into timber length logs to be hauled to a mill for lumber. The stumps of the felled trees were to be blasted out with dynamite and the holes filled with earth. The end result was to form a parklike corridor along both sides of the road, the full length of the burned area.

The company had a tough Swede in charge of the dynamite blasting whom Dan observed with envy. Dynamite had a great appeal for Dan, and he had done lots of blasting in Michigan. The Swede would load fifteen or twenty stumps to be blasted out and then blow a bugle in an awful distorted rendition of a fox hunt fanfare, and yell, "Firing a hole," and everyone would duck for cover. The Swede would count each blast on his fingers as they occurred to make sure all the charges had gone off. But more often than not, he would miscount and yell, "That's all," only to have a couple more belated charges occur with stumps flying in the air while everyone ducked behind trees again. Dan was greatly amused by the Swede's mistaken counting of the blasts, but some of the other workmen were not so amused by it.

One day Dan was offering John a helping hand at cutting brush, and was getting a first-hand experience of just how tough those fire-hardened bushes were, when he announced, "John, there has to be an easier way to do this. Let's just burn it down." Without warning or asking the foreman's advice, Dan set fire to a clump of dry manzanita brush. There was almost an explosion of flame that began spreading very quickly. Workmen ran from every direction to put out the fire. They barely got it under control before starting another massive forest fire. The McNutt Company probably determined right then not to give Dan another job. The boys finished the contract and the family was terminated, losing an excellent opportunity to continue working during the now, very deep, economic depression.

As a last joy ride in the old Nash before going back to Eugene from "Walk and Push Hill," Dan drove the boys up to Crater Lake—only a few miles distance. At that time there was yet no rim road around the lake, so they came upon the lake at the end of a graveled approach road. One moment they were driving through dense forests, and then suddenly before them was the crater with a lake down in it that looked like a deep blue sapphire jewel. John had never seen anything like it and was emotionally overcome by the beauty of the scene. When told that the lake was about seven miles across, he was astonished, for in the crystal-clear air, it appeared to be no more than a mile at the most. They stood at the edge of the cliff with a two-thousand-foot drop below to the lake level and silently marveled at the scene. There were as yet no well-established trails down into the crater, so they made no attempt to descend down into it.

Exercising his authority, as head of the family, Dan again pocketed all the money the boys had made at "Walk and Push Hill," and as usual made a decision as to what the family would do next. He returned to Eugene, Oregon, picked up Mary and their few household items, and drove to Gold Hill, Oregon, where Dan's idea was to locate the homestead property that had once belonged to Mary's relatives many years before, and which had been returned to county ownership for delinquent taxes. There was no particular reason for the move except that the family was out of work again and the prospects for another job were almost nonexistent.

The name of the village, "Gold Hill," was intriguing to Dan and whetted his curiosity. He probably had the notion of just squatting on the homestead property till a new job opportunity arose. But by this time, early autumn of 1929, job losses across the nation were increasing at an alarming rate. President Hoover's administration was frustrated and bewildered by the economic collapse, but publicly was assuring the populace that all was well, that there was really no problem. Then on October 29, 1929, the New York stock market plummeted and lost fifteen billion dollars of value in just one stunning week.

It was at this time that began the most hopeless and impoverished period to ever again occur in the Macdonald family, and in the nation as a whole, years of hardship, of hunger, of wretched poverty—the years of the Great Depression that never really ended till a decade later at the beginning of World War II. Yet for John, and also for many Americans, these poverty years were perhaps the finest years of our history, inspiring the very best in human relations, of people helping people with kindness and compassion, and perhaps also that may have been the best years in the history of our civic institutions, bending but not breaking, experimenting and adjusting to the challenges of the failed economy.

10

When the family arrived in Gold Hill, Dan drove to the Jackson County court house and located county maps showing the homestead land. It was at the headwaters of a stream called Sardine Creek, a small tributary of the Rogue River. The creek entrance to the river was downstream about a mile from the town of Gold Hill. The town was a little impoverished village of perhaps three hundred people. There was a grocery store and combined hardware where locally mined gold was purchased from the miners, and there was a scattering of service stations and cafés. The town's only industry was a large cement quarry.

Sardine Creek had a county road that took one upstream several miles past cattle ranches and small farms, till the creek branched into a north and south fork. The north fork terminated at a famous landmark anomaly in the earth's gravitational field. There was an ancient miner's shack there where tourists were mystified by balls that seemed to run uphill, and plumb bobs that seem to hang at an angle instead of straight toward the center of the earth.

But it was at the head of the south fork of the stream where Mary's relatives' property was, about eight miles upstream of the creek fork. In fact the land and house was at the very top of a mountain pass that dropped off into a wide valley, named Sam's Valley. The road to the property stopped short of reaching there by about a mile, so to reach the place, one had to drive to the end of the road and then hike into the mountains another mile.

The road itself was a barely functional logging trail that had not been used, except by an occasional gold miner, for years. En route were quite a number of log bridges covered with earth that were of questionable safety.

About a mile upstream from the creek fork, Dan found a large family of rustic people, living in an equally rustic house, by the name of King. Mr. King was a flamboyant character, with a flaming red bristling beard and equally flaming red hair. Mr. King was about fifty years old and obviously as tough as nails. Mrs. King was a ragged, unkempt woman, most notable for the blandness of her personality. She seemed to be relegated, by both her husband and children, down to the very bottom of the social ladder in the King family, perhaps only a step higher than the goats she attended. The only time she spoke was when the terror of her husband was mitigated by his absence.

There were four children, the youngest of them being a five-year-old child who already smoked and rolled his own cigarettes. The children were all illiterate. None of the children had attended school. Mr. King's total family sustenance was rooted in wresting a living from the natural resources of the area, hunting and fishing, a garden, milk goats, and gold mining. But if Mr. King was deficient in academia, he was highly educated in practical knowledge of how to exploit every natural resource at his disposal, and as a consequence, the economic depression had little effect on their livelihood.

For meat they shot deer, raised goats, and trapped migratory salmon in the creek; for vegetables they grew a garden; they had fruit trees; for money they mined gold. When Dan observed how the Kings lived without depending upon any kind of salary, it greatly impressed him, and the novel idea of mining gold was especially intriguing, for this would be a way for his family to work their way through the depression. Also there began to lurk, at the back of Dan's mind, a romantic dream: perhaps they could find a deposit of gold that would make them rich—who knows.

It should be an established rule that whenever one is listening to people expounding on their gold-mining accomplishments, the amount of riches reportedly acquired should be mentally discounted by half or more, for almost without exception, they exaggerate. There is something in the human psyche that compels exhibitionism when talking about gold. Mr. King was especially articulate about the subject and could spin endless tales by the hour about his exploits in gold-mining, and Dan listened with rapt attention. The poverty in which the Kings lived did not seem to square well with the gold wealth he had supposedly mined, but Dan took no notice of the incongruity. As head of the family, Dan quickly made up his mind that the Macdonalds would now all mine placer gold for a living from Sardine Creek.

Dan inquired from King if he knew of a cabin they could move into. Mr. King obliged by telling him about an empty cabin about a mile downstream from the Kings' house that the Macdonalds could occupy.

In the following days, Dan acquired a short course of instruction from Mr. King on how to go about placer mining: the heavy gold, King pointed out, tends to collect at the inside of sharp curves in the stream bed, or in deep crevices in the bedrock beneath the creek bed. Shovel off the top soil, called over-burden, Dan was instructed, and dig down into the deeper undisturbed gravel bed of the stream. Place a shovel full of what you think is gold-bearing gravel into a gold pan and throw out the coarse stones. Swirl the pan to settle the gold to the bottom, and gently lap water over the side of the pan to wash away the sand. Continue this operation till the gold becomes visible in the bottom of the pan. This was the way to find a suitable place to set up a mining claim.

The next step was to build sluice boxes, wooden troughs about eight to ten feet long, and eight to ten inches wide. The sluice boxes were to be made tapered at the ends so each would fit into the next in a chain of sluice boxes. Placed within the downstream box would be a rack of wooden riffles, short pieces of lath wood held together by a frame, over which a stream of water from the creek was to be directed to flow through the sluice boxes. Under the riffles was stretched a piece of burlap sacking to snag the finer gold that otherwise might wash away with the force of the flowing water. When all this was set up, the miner shoveled what he hoped was gold-bearing gravel into the upstream sluice box and the flowing water washed it down over the riffles where the heavy gold settled, and the fine gold was caught in the burlap sacking beneath the riffles.

It was a crude technology, and probably a good portion of the gold simply washed straight through past the riffle and was lost. Actually it was technology straight out of the 1849 western Gold Rush movement.

After a day of mining, the water flow is diverted out of the sluice boxes, the riffle rack and burlap sacking removed, and all the sand and gold contents rinsed into a gold pan. Then, very carefully, the excess sand was panned away to leave the concentrated gold and a little so-called black sand—actually particles of heavy iron. The day's collection of gold and black sand was placed in a jar and each succeeding day's accumulation added to the whole. At the end of a week, the contents of the jar would be dumped back into a gold pan, and again carefully panned a bit to remove as much of the black sand as possible. Any nuggets would be picked out and put into a vial for safe keeping. One tends to think of nuggets as perhaps the size of birds' eggs, but the real nuggets are more apt to be the size of ants' eggs—at least that is what the Macdonalds found. Very rarely they might find one the size of the head of a match.

After the nuggets, if any, are removed, there comes the really sophisticated technology to separate the fine gold from any remaining black sand. A globule of quicksilver or mercury is dropped into the gold pan, and stirred about with the gold so they contact each other. When this is done, the gold bonds to the mercury and every tiny particle of gold becomes enmeshed in the globule of quicksilver.

This mercury and gold mixture is called an amalgam. The amalgam is now removed from the gold pan and placed in the bottom of a skillet, usually the same skillet the miner uses to cook his hot cakes and fry his bacon in. Now a medium-sized potato is cut in half, and one half of the potato is hollowed out with a spoon to form a neat cavity. The hollowed potato cavity is placed down over the amalgam in the bottom of the skillet and the pan is heated over a fire. The miner stands cautiously upwind of the firing to make sure he doesn't breathe any of the fumes given off by the heated mercury, for it can be very toxic.

In this crude miniature retort, the heated mercury forms gas and is driven off from the amalgam, leaving a little pile of unadulterated gold. When the mercury gas contacts the wet cool inside of the potato cavity, it condenses back into many tiny globules that cling to the inside of the potato. The pure gold can then be transferred into a vial for safe keeping, and the tiny mercury globules scraped out of the potato, gathered together, and put back into a bottle again for the next amalgam.

The gold could be sold at a grocery store in the village of Gold Hill, or it could be taken to Grant's Pass, a few miles north, and sold to a bank. In either case it was discounted somewhat, depending upon where it had come from, as different areas' gold was somewhat different in purity. Some native gold contains silver. The going price at that time was twelve dollars per ounce. At the time of writing, the price of gold is about 350 dollars an ounce.

Dan invested in a gold pan, picks and shovels, and some lumber to make sluice boxes. The equipment was transported about a mile upstream from the Kings' diggings, and optimistically set up for placer mining in Sardine Creek. The family settled into the vacant cabin about a mile downstream from the Kings, so that each day's trek to the Macdonalds' mining claim was about a two-mile hike past the Kings' house.

Unfortunately whoever designed the fireplace in the cabin the Macdonalds occupied had not been very skilled at the job, so that as much smoke filled the cabin as went up the chimney. The autumn weather was beginning to get cold, and it was necessary to immediately gather firewood to heat the one-room cabin and to cook with. In that area about the only trees available were madrone, a very wet sap saturated tree that would barely burn. It would have taken months for the madrone to dry enough to make good firewood, and they had to use it right away. The wood produced very little heat and great quantities of steamy smoke that filled the cabin. But they made the most of it.

The gold mining turned out to be even more unsatisfactory than their cold, smoke-filled cabin home. The family found that by putting in very long hard work days of ten to twelve hours of labor shoveling creek gravel into the sluice boxes and scraping and digging out nooks and crevices in the bedrock bottom of the creek bed, the four of them could gather about a dime's worth of gold in a good day, and much less in a bad day. Everyone was discouraged but Dan.

Dan just assumed that they had not found the right spot, and so each discouraging few days, he kept moving to a new site, but each new site proved to be as bad as the others. In the meantime they were using up what little money they had saved while working for the McNutt Company. Very soon they were short on rations, not that the boys had ever had really enough food even in the good times to satisfy their youthful appetites.

Adding to their misery, the weather was now turning very cold and the clothing they had brought out with them from Michigan was becoming ragged and worn. The soles of John's shoes wore completely through from the grinding gravel in the creek and had to be abandoned. In desperation he found an old pair of discarded rubber boots in a trash dump that had holes in the soles, but were better than his shoes. John wrapped his feet in rags inside the discarded boots and went on working with constantly wet cold feet.

In exploring the countryside, the Macdonalds discovered that along the Rogue River between Gold Hill and Grant's Pass, there was a number of large pear orchards. The economy was so bad that it didn't pay the farmers to have the fruit picked. Consequently, the entire season's fruit crop matured and fell to the ground. Dan found that they could drive into the orchards and pick up off the ground all the pears they wanted. Thereafter, for a while at least before the fruit rotted, their very limited food supply was bolstered with pears.

After the pears ran out, the only food that the tiny amount of gold that they were mining could buy was the most elementary staples of flour and potatoes. For breakfast Mary would boil water with a bit of salt in it and sift flour into the boiling water to form a sort of porridge that she called, "minute pudding."

Actually it was the same formula used to make wallpaper paste. There was not enough food to make a lunch at noon, and supper consisted of one or two boiled potatoes and sometimes a biscuit. The extremely hard work of mining for ten to twelve hours a day, seven days a week, produced ravenous appetites that could never be appeased. It became too much for Dan, so he just began staying in the cabin all day, letting the boys do all the work.

One morning the boys were walking to the diggings, and as they were passing a cabin where some woodcutters lived, the door of the shack flew open and some object was flung out on the ground. Spot, the family dog, sniffed the air, and then dashed to the cabin and scooped up a badly burned pancake. The poor animal was starving. There was immediate pandemonium. All three boys pounced on the dog and tore the pancake away from her. Privation was causing tempers to flare. Dave and Ron quarreled over whether they should allow the dog to have a piece of the precious burnt pancake, or whether they should just divide it up among themselves. Reluctantly, the dog won a tiny piece. The boys were elated that they were so lucky as to unexpectedly obtain this bite of food to eat, which was essentially garbage.

It was soon noticeable to the boys that their stepmother, Mary, who was grossly overweight, and was staying in the cabin all day with Dan, was not losing any weight from deprivation. The circumstantial evidence of her cheating set up severe resentments. Dan did not consume much food at any time, so they cast no blame on him, but it appeared to the boys that their father expected them to go on mining gold and undergoing starvation while he stayed in the cabin with Mary, and she was eating enough food to sustain her overweight fat.

En route to their mining claim each morning, the boys hiked past the Kings' apple orchard, and in hungry desperation, they would pick apples and eat them. One day Dan returned from visiting the Kings visibly shaken. Mr. King had threatened that he or his sons were going to shoot anyone caught stealing apples from his orchard. The Kings were a tough family, so Dan took the threat seriously. Mr. King carried a pistol in a holster with him everywhere, and his sons all carried hunting rifles. Although it seemed ridiculous to believe that anyone would kill a person for an apple, Dan was very worried and started to look for a different place to live.

A number of miles upstream from the Kings, at the very top of the mountain pass, was the homestead land that Dan had come to Gold Hill to find. The land had an old well-built cabin on it that they considered moving into, but unfortunately the logging road ended a good mile short of the cabin.

What they needed was a cabin on the logging road so they could drive back and forth to town for supplies. Fortuitously, about a mile down the mountain pass from the homestead, at the very upper end of the Sardine Creek logging road, there was another abandoned cabin. A decision was made to move there at once before a murder took place over stolen apples. They also quickly set about reestablishing the family mining operation at this new location, for one place was about as good—or bad as another. The new location was completely isolated from any other neighbors by miles of barely driveable logging trails, and was in a deeply forested area.

This lonely shack of a cabin was now to become John's home for the next four years of painful hunger, bitter privation, and almost total isolation, all of it occurring in his early teen years when normal children are attending school and learning skills for maturity.

The mining here proved to be just as bad as it was

downstream, but Dan still continued to insist that they would make a rich strike before long and their problems would be over. His sight was failing and he would often pick up a yellow pebble from the creek, bring it to John, and ask pleadingly, "Is this a nugget, John?" And John would have to answer, "No, it's just a rock." Yet never did Dan give up faith that in the next mining site, or the next shovel of gravel, they would turn up a bonanza.

Dan was even told by local people that the probability of finding any quantity of gold was negligible because the stream had been thoroughly mined in the forty-nine Gold Rush, and then mined again by the Chinese after they had finished building the continental railroad to the West. None of the information had the slightest effect of discouraging Dan from assuming he would eventually make a rich gold strike.

The family tried to make themselves as comfortable as possible in the new cabin, given the circumstances. Somehow they had acquired an old radio that could be operated off of the power from the six-volt car battery. However, if they used the radio very much, it ran the car battery down and then they could not start the car to drive to town. Brother Dave, with his penchant for invention, decided to do something about this. He built a water wheel and installed it in the creek as a source of power. On the side of the water wheel, he built a crude wooden pulley, and he made a pulley belt out of strips of braided raw deer hide. The belt carried mechanical power from the water wheel to the pulley on the car generator, which was removed from the car and mounted on a platform at the side of the creek. This device turned the car generator fast enough to produce a couple of amperes of charging current, just enough to recharge the battery. Thereafter they had the comfort of at least listening to the radio at night to determine what was going on in the world, even though the news was all very discouraging.

The Hoover administration was continuing to make optimistic statements that the nation's economy was basically sound. For families like the Macdonalds, the message came across as so false that it provoked bitter anger. Worse yet the federal government was not providing any kind of emergency measures to relieve the suffering and privation of countless unemployed citizens. This was the time before unemployment insurance, before the time of Social Security, before the time of food stamps, before the time of homeless shelters. The federal government had no agencies or programs of any kind to mitigate the hardships of its citizens.

Dave's improvisation for charging the car battery so they could use it to power the radio was a great success, but even that was soon to indirectly fall victim to their desperate circumstances. Their dog Spot, who was slowly starving to death, one night ate the rawhide belt that ran the generator, effectively cutting off news from the rest of the world.

By now brother Ron was taking the rifle, which they had brought out from Michigan with them, for a daily hunt for whatever animal he could kill for meat. He had already managed to bag a deer from which the deer-hide belt was made that ran the car generator. Sometimes Ron would find a porcupine to shoot. At another time it was a large owl. Both were delicious. The owl tasted like chicken. He shot a skunk, carefully dressed it out, and they ate it. The skunk had a flavor resembling pork, and they rendered the fat to use as butter.

Ron shot silver-gray squirrels and they made stew out of them. The dog ate the hides and entrails of all these animals, even driving quantities of quills into her muzzle in an attempt to eat the porcupine hide—she was so pitifully starved.

One day brother Ron shot a gray squirrel and the creature died clinging to the top of a fir tree. Ron refused to lose his quarry, so he climbed the tree to retrieve the squirrel. He was wearing an old black sweater at the time, and unknown to him, another hunter was happening by. The hunter heard the sounds of branches snapping in the tree, and as he looked upward, Ron's black sweatered arm reached around the side of the tree trunk in view of the hunter. The startled man thought, *Wow, a black bear.* He cocked his 30-30 rifle and sighted in, but decided at the last minute not to pull the trigger because it would only wound the animal. About that time Ron's face appeared from around the side of the tree and the hunter was aghast at how close he had come to shooting. Ron and the hunter soon got acquainted. The hunter's name was John Paine, and he lived about six miles away down in Sam's Valley.

Mr. Paine was an amiable man and he invited Ron to return with him to visit his Sam's Valley home. The valley had to be approached by climbing to the top of the saddle back out of which Sardine Creek headwaters flowed, and then down a steep trail on the other side into a wide arroyo, which carried the stream bed of another creek.

Mr. Paine had an extended family of cousins and brothers all living nearby, and there was also a small community of farmers and gold miners near his rancho. Several miles down the valley, there was even a little grammar school, a grocery store, and a post office. Ron observed with great interest that the Paines' house was served with electric power, and that Paine had a battery charger. Ron quickly made a deal to get the Nash car battery charged at Mr. Paine's house. The Macdonalds had not been able to drive into town since the dog had eaten the vital rawhide belt used in charging the car battery. Mr. Paine was agreeable to the arrangement, and Ron returned triumphantly to the cabin on Sardine Creek to announce his scheme.

The very next morning, Ron and John contrived a two-man sling from which the battery could be suspended for transporting it to Sam's Valley on a six-mile hike over the mountain pass and down perhaps a thousand feet of elevation, on a crude trail of thirty percent or more grade, and then out onto the valley floor to Paine's house. The battery was left for overnight charging, and they returned on the six-mile hike back again to Sardine Creek. Next day they made the twelve-mile round trip again to bring the charged battery back, for a total of twenty-four miles of climbing and hiking to get the battery charged before they could get ready to drive into town for their meager supplies. But the next step in the process of driving into town could be even more arduous.

They found it was not wise to just install the battery in the car and step on the starter, for after the Nash had been setting out in the damp weather for three weeks or a month, it would just run the battery down again. A large amount of preliminary work had to be done first. All the ignition wiring and the distributor had to be carefully dried out first. Then it was propitious to push the car down a hill with the gears engaged, thus turning the engine mechanically instead of using the starter to turn it, for that would again put too heavy a drain on the battery. So the job of starting the car engine for a trip into town had to be approached with great caution and planning because if it were not, it involved another twenty-four miles of hiking for the boys to obtain another recharge of the battery.

After carefully drying all the ignition wiring and priming the cylinders with gasoline, the car was pushed to the brow of the first hill heading down the Sardine Creek logging trail. Dan then got into the car, turned on the ignition, and everyone pushed the car downhill with the engine in gear, hoping for favorable results. But usually the engine would not start on the first hill and it would roll clear to the bottom with only a few preliminary chug-chugs. In that event Dan would get out a set of blocks and rope tackle, attach one pulley to a tree and the other pulley to the front axle, and with everyone pulling on the rope, they would gradually work the car up to the top of the next hill from which they could push it down again, in gear, for a second try.

Sometimes it took three or more hills and the larger part of a day's work to start the car before they could drive to town. Later in the winter, heavy snow prevented them from driving the car at all. Then Dave built a toboggan sled for carrying in supplies. The boys harnessed themselves to the sled and each trip into town was an arduous twenty-four-mile round trip journey of pulling the toboggan up and down steep mountain grades.

By 1930 Jackson County was issuing emergency food to those people who were completely destitute. The Macdonald family certainly qualified. So thereafter, when they got into town, they could often get a small box of food that would last perhaps for five days, after which they were hungry again. But at least it was better than what the federal government was doing, which was nothing at all. The American people were getting very angry at the Hoover administration. To make matters worse, there were stories being told of the agriculture department buying up hundreds of hogs and destroying the meat, of buying up milk and dumping it down sewers, of destroying potatoes, all in a vain attempt to prop up prices. The theory was advanced that overproduction was depressing the economy. In this insane response, the nation was a cornucopia of food, yet large numbers of people were starving.

As time went on, the boys became ever more discouraged with gold mining, but Dan kept insisting that they could strike it rich any day now.

The work days were long, cold, wet, exhausting, and the pangs of hunger incessant. One fell into a sort of dream world in which the mind wandered off into inventing imaginary meals and imaginary visions of rest from the endless toil. John welcomed each night of sleep as the only respite from hunger, aching muscles, and cold wet feet.

One day Ron suggested that they should hold out some of the gold they were mining, and he would secretly hike into town and buy whatever amount of food they could with it, to consume for themselves. Each day for a week or more, they craftily secreted away tiny nuggets till they had enough gold to make the long trip worthwhile. Dan would not miss Ron at the diggings because he and Mary were staying in the cabin all day anyway while the boys worked. Ron made the trip to Gold Hill and back with less than fifty cents worth of gold, which he traded for a large sack of cookies and a box of raisins. Despite his own hunger, he brought the entire tiny food supply back with him and the three boys divided it evenly to the last raisin.

By now Dave and Ron began to consider disobeying their father and to just leave Dan to his gold mining to seek their own livelihood elsewhere. John was only thirteen years old and too immature to leave home yet. Dave suggested that they should hitch-hike to Milwaukee, Wisconsin, and go to their maternal grandfather, Jim Campbell. Perhaps he would help them.

The two boys confronted their father with the plan. Dan was astonished that they were so dissatisfied and shocked at the plan, for he disliked the Campbells intensely. Dan begged them not to go to the Campbells; it would humiliate him. There was a very emotional confrontation in which the boys insisted they were going to leave home. Their lives could not possibly be any worse than it was mining gold.

So on a spring day in 1930, in spite of Dan's pleading, brothers Ron and Dave left Sardine Creek for adventures of their own and a new life. This left John and his father and stepmother isolated in the lonely cabin on Sardine Creek, without money, without food, and without hope as far as John was concerned. Their prospects for survival were indeed dismal.

11

When Ron and Dave left to pursue their own living elsewhere, Dan felt abandoned. He had been depending on them to support the family, as a farmer would depend on a team of horses. It did not seem morally right that they should abandon their responsibilities to him and to each other. Dan's mind-set was that, as a family, the father should direct and control, and the sons and daughters should obey. That was how all family affairs should be conducted, he thought, for that had been the accepted standard of behavior that he had experienced, in the rural America that he had grown up in. Only through the sacrifice of individualism to the unity of the family could there be enough energy generated to combat the rigors of rural living in the semi-frontier life he had experienced. But rural America was rapidly becoming urban America, and Dan's vision had not kept pace with the change. Now individualism was being stressed. Ideally, each child was only to be guided by parents, and each child was to be encouraged to develop his own inherent gifts within a more loosely defined family unit. Dan just could not understand what had taken place.

It was obvious to Dan that he and John, by themselves, could not mine enough gold to maintain themselves. But still he had not given up all hope, for there persevered in the back of his mind that if only the mining could be done on a large enough scale, it would be profitable. For example, there was a cattle rancher down at the mouth of Sardine Creek, who spent his winters hydraulic mining, a means of moving and processing huge amounts of gold-bearing gravel.

The Smiths' mining operation seemed to be successful, but no one knew how much money they were making. Hydraulic mining was an idea that was lying fallow in Dan's mind while he was conjuring up some temporary way to meet his immediate needs for sustenance.

Dan wrote to his daughter, Helen, who was living in Florida, working as a housekeeper for a pittance of a salary, and asked if she could send a monthly sum of money to help sustain the diminished family. Helen kindly agreed to help and wrote back that she could send ten dollars per month. In the live-in arrangement that she was working at, in a private home, the ten dollars may have been half of her salary. The ten dollars a month was a big help, especially when added to the occasional box of relief food from the government. For the remainder of their needs, Dan came up with another idea: he and John would cut firewood from the abundant fir trees surrounding them. They would transport the firewood to Medford with the old Nash pulling the trailer, and sell it to whomever they could. The trees, of course, were owned by a timber company, but that small theft was brushed off with the self-fulfilling view that the trees were just growing there as a gift of nature, so who would care.

Together they cut and split wood, filling the back of the car and the trailer to capacity, and set out for Medford. The effort was mildly successful, but it was very hard on the car.

It soon became clear that if the transmission of the car was destroyed they would be in very serious trouble, so cutting firewood was abandoned. But by one means and another, they managed to get through the spring and summer of 1931, yet it was so difficult that Dan soon tired of this endless struggling for enough food to sustain them, and tired of the blandness of their diet of bread, beans, and potatoes. One day he announced to John that they would no longer go without meat. Range cattle were wandering about grazing all through their area of Sardine Creek. They would simply shoot a young steer.

Dan and John equipped themselves with shovels, axe, and knife, and the family rifle, and made a sortie into the woods behind their cabin to find a herd of grazing cattle. Dan selected a nice fat specimen and shot it. Together they skinned the animal and buried the hide and entrails in a shallow hole, to destroy the evidence of the slaughter. They cut the body into quarters and hauled it back to the house in a wheelbarrow. There Dan, using as much speed as possible, carved the flesh from the carcass and then burned the bones. Mary cut the meat up into manageable portions, packed it in mason jars, and canned it. Dan cut an opening in the kitchen floor of the cabin and stored the jars under there, then made a removable panel in the floor that was barely visible. The whole procedure was accomplished in just two self-satisfying days. But like many crimes that are committed, they had overlooked a weak point in the plan, the family dog.

Very soon, unknown to the family, Spot sniffed out the burial hole of the entrails and hide, and dug it all up. A few days later, a local rancher and his wife came riding through on saddle horses and stopped at the cabin. They were friendly and chatted amiably. The lady asked if she could come in the house and have a drink of water. Dan obliged and they left. There was something about the visit that raised a feeling of anxiety in John's mind.

John set out one morning a couple of days later, carrying the family rifle, to hunt for whatever creature turned up in his path. As he was walking down the logging trail, he heard a car coming. A car in that isolated place was a very unusual event. A pickup truck soon appeared from around a bend. John recognized the occupants at once as the Smiths. They pulled up to a quick stop and shouted at him in alarm.

"Hey, kid, throw that rifle in the bushes," they yelled.

John was dumfounded at the demand and stood mutely frozen. Very quickly a car load of state police came into view and stopped.

One of the officers said, "I'll take that rifle, boy."

John handed it over and the officer removed the cartridges from it and stowed it in the police car.

"What are you shooting?" the officers demanded.

John was flustered and the first thing that came to his mind he blurted out, "Grouse." It happened that there were a few rarely seen grouse in the area, but there was not even a hunting season for the birds, and besides, to ever hit one with a rifle would be a small miracle. So John's answer to their demand was almost ridiculous.

Since he had no birds, there was no offense committed anyway, but he had accidentally given them a disarming answer. If he was hunting grouse, it would seem to indicate that the family was in need of meat and therefore it was unlikely that they had rustled a beef steer.

Behind the state police car, another car now drove up and in it were the rancher and his wife who had visited the Macdonalds' cabin a few days before. The police took John in their car up to the cabin, and without any search warrant, they searched every nook and corner as well as all the adjacent area for beef or by-products of beef butchering. The only thing they found was a piece of liver in a pan. Mary lied, telling them she had bought it in the market.

The police questioned Dan and Mary closely, and then took John outside, apart from his parents, and questioned him. John denied that he knew anything about the dug-up cow hide. After a harried hour of interrogation, in which the police could find no evidence of a crime, they took with them the confiscated rifle and everyone left. When John reviewed the incident in his mind, it became clear that the Smiths had pitied the obvious plight that the Macdonalds were in, and had tried in vain to get John to discard the rifle to prevent the police from confiscating it. It was an act of kindness such as he had rarely experienced.

All during the time that the search was going on, Mary had seated her broad buttocks on a chair over the secret panel in the floor, under which the beef was hidden, and displayed an expression of outraged indignity at this intrusion of privacy.

A few days after the raid, Dan reclaimed the rifle. He never again mustered the courage to try cattle rustling in spite of the fact that for a couple of months thereafter they enjoyed succulent beef to supplement their sparse diet. It was not a crime that evoked much sense of guilt, for the pangs of severe hunger recognize no laws of ownership to food.

John gradually became so distressed by their family circumstances that he began withdrawing into himself and stopped talking to anyone. What was there to talk about except the disaster that was occurring in their lives? His mind had become encapsulated like a dried seed just lying in the soil waiting for the drought to end. Each day he would walk out into the forest by himself. He always took the family rifle along, ostensibly to hunt game for provender, but he was not the skilled hunter that his brother Ron was. He rarely killed an animal, and he actually disliked being a hunter. His sympathy was with the animals. Often he morbidly thought how easy it would be to turn the rifle upon himself.

Occasionally John would visit the site of an old tumbled-down cabin in one of the arroyos of Sardine Creek valley.

There were several ancient apple trees there that were gnarled and diseased, but still producing a few apples. One morning he had come early and was sitting very still in the sun to absorb the morning rays. Suddenly a coyote appeared in the apple orchard without the rustle of a leaf or the crackle of a twig. His presence was almost ghostly. John watched the coyote intently as the animal sat on its haunches in the sun, clearly enjoying the morning warmth. After a time the coyote stood and stretched, and began battering playfully at fallen apples. He would knock an apple a yard or more away and then pounce on it like it was a creature of prey, grab it in his mouth and toss it in the air, then dash about like a puppy. If the coyote knew John was there, he paid no attention to him at all, and was obviously enjoying his own game, which went on for about half an hour. Then suddenly, silently, he was gone, vanished in the deep forest shadows as quietly as he had come out of it.

The coyote's game was such an impressive display that John began returning to the apple orchard daily, hoping to catch sight of the animal again. Sure enough, every now and then, the coyote would return, paying no attention to John who was only a few feet away observing. It was as if they had an understanding to be agreeable neighbors resigned to the quiet comradeship in each other's presence. John ate wormy apples while awaiting the coyote to appear, and sometimes for several days he would not make a return visit, but only to reappear again unexpectedly for a morning frolic, and then trot into the forest as mysteriously as a ghost.

The lonely isolation of John's life after his brothers left evoked a deep feeling of hopelessness and depression.

There was a sense of abandonment by fellow humans, and a sense of reattachment to the world of nature, a feeling that the coyote and the wilds of the Oregon forest were his only reality, and that people were intruders in it. The only two people in his life, his stepmother and father, were becoming alien to him even. His stepmother's presence incurred fear and loathing. If she was a prototype of humanity, then humanity may as well be abandoned.

John's father presented an even more difficult problem. His feeling toward his father was one of duty combined with need of nurture. Their only communication was contained within Dan's self-directed agenda of expecting his son to do whatever was necessary to carry out his goals. John felt that instead of being his father's son, he had become his father's tool. Rarely did Dan chat with John in such a way as to establish mutual respect. Dan was so self-directed that his tendency was to just use whatever person was at hand to fulfill his priorities of the moment. The needs of people serving Dan never entered his mind. He was not selfish, but he was thoughtless and responding to the terrible struggles of his own childhood that had taught him to survive by assertiveness.

In his lonely circumstances, it became necessary for John to reach into himself to develop strange methods of mental sustenance. He discovered something interesting about the cabin on the homestead land that had brought Dan to Gold Hill and Sardine Creek.

The cabin was about a mile distant from where they were living, and at the very top of a mountain pass. It was in a place that was so isolated that it had remained undisturbed by vandals, almost as the owner had left it years ago. The interior walls were papered with circa 1800 newspapers. John found he could entertain himself by the hour reading these ancient papers. All the stories and even the ads and pictures told him about the current events in the area three quarters of a century ago. Then John learned that there was a Jackson County branch library about eight miles down Sardine Creek, in a chicken rancher's house. Thereafter he hiked each week the sixteen-mile round trip to check out books to read, reestablishing the reading habit he had acquired in his Michigan grammar school, which seemed an eternity back in time.

Books not only helped mitigate the loneliness, but they also became an educational supplement. He loved reading about science and physics, and he pored over endless novels. He discovered there is no better way to learn about human relations than through the minds of good authors. He was forever afterward extremely grateful to the American library system, and to the Jackson County Library in particular. That library had come close to saving his sanity that year in 1931.

Even Dan began getting books from the branch library, but his were about how to assay gold ore, and he started rambling about through the mountains, chipping off bits of mica-impregnated rock that he was sure were gold, and bringing it home to John to examine.

Through a county relief agency, Dan finally got a temporary job in an adjoining valley doing some kind of forestry work for a while. He worked at it but a very short time before he quit, preferring to continue the endless quest for gold. With Sister Helen's help, they were barely managing to survive.

The year of 1931 was slipping by, with John having almost no social contact with any living person except his father and stepmother and the kindly branch librarian. He grew increasingly shy and withdrawn. He was ashamed of his own ignorance and lack of education, ashamed of his ragged clothing, ashamed of his backwoods life. He began to feel that he did not have the human standards required to socialize with anyone. His only comforts were the dog Spot, the woods and wildlife including a furtive coyote, and reading endless books. He became withdrawn to the point of slinking away and hiding if a stranger came to their cabin. He was feeling increasingly suicidal, and if people spoke to him kindly, he would cry, being emotionally overwhelmed by the strange advent of kindness.

Then about mid-year of 1931, an odd event took place that had ramifications for John so far beyond imagination that no one could have predicted the consequences that transpired from it. The pet collie dog, who was starving all through the years of privation, had developed a sharpening of her survival abilities. She never became a predator, but she learned how to cunningly steal food.

Every now and then, someone with a little grubstake would come up Sardine Creek and set up a campsite while they prospected for gold. Spot would seek out these campsites and carefully watch if anyone was around. When the camp was vacant, she would steal their food supply. One day she came home dragging an enormous side of bacon. John took it from her. She was a gentle dog. As hungry as she was, she actually seemed pleased to give away her plunder. Dan carefully cut the bacon away from the rind, and for the next several days, she had bits of bacon rind mixed with her boiled potato peelings that was her daily ration. The family of course ate every morsel of the bacon itself. But what was more important, Mary carefully saved all of the bacon fat fried out of the bacon, to later use as a substitute for butter to spread on bread. During the following weeks, the daily menu consisted of mostly bacon grease buttered sandwiches, and Mary indulged herself generously as she usually did, slathering the grease onto bread and consuming it.

One day Mary became suddenly ill and in great pain. It was clear that she had to have immediate medical attention. She began moaning and even screaming with pain. Dan put her in the car and drove hurriedly to Medford where doctors diagnosed it as an acute gall-bladder attack. She would have to be operated on at once to remove the organ. Dan reluctantly left Mary in the hospital and returned to the Sardine Creek cabin. Isolated as he and John were, they had no way to keep in touch with the hospital, and only limited gasoline to drive back and forth to see Mary.

Dan waited two days and then drove back to Medford to see what had happened to her. He found the operation had been a complete success and she was recovering nicely.

John, who had taken the brunt of Mary's cruelty for so many years, found it difficult to be very sympathetic about her illness, especially since she had undoubtedly brought it on herself by eating excessive amounts of bacon grease. All through the years of their privation, she alone had maintained a ponderous flabby body weight, indicating she was overeating and thereby cheating the boys from getting their fair share of the limited food supply. Mary kept an absolute dominance over the food at all times, scantily rationing it to the boys while fixing her and Dan's food separately, and in secret, so the boys could not know what she and Dan were consuming.

At the time of the hospital visit, Dan got a bright idea. He went to the local broadcasting station studio in Medford and told them his circumstances, that his wife was in the hospital recovering from an operation, and he was going to be out of touch with her, miles away on Sardine Creek. He asked if they could announce over the radio how she was doing, and in this way, he could get word about her. They kindly agreed to do just that and a time was set up for him to listen to the radio. And sure enough, right on schedule, they made an announcement for a few days that she was doing fine.

Then there were no further announcements. Dan waited about a week before he could get in to Medford again to visit her. He and John walked up the corridor to her hospital room only to find that she wasn't there any longer. Dan inquired for her at the desk, and was stunned when the nurse told him she was dead. She had been recovering nicely when she developed an embolism, a blood clot causing sudden death.

The abrupt termination of Mary's life was so astounding that John couldn't believe it. She had always appeared to him to be so all powerful, in her dominance over him, that he had regarded her as an unending indestructible living force. Suddenly a time had come when this ogre of a woman could not hurt him again. He felt happy, but guilty for being happy about someone's death. Then, some time later, he learned that he was wrong about that first vision of release he anticipated after she died, that she still had the power, even after death, to cast her baneful spell over his personality.

John had never believed that his father had actually loved this woman, because for John, she was utterly unlovable. Yet obviously Dan was deeply grieved by her passing, and that surprised John that his father really cared that much for her. Mary's death evoked such mental confusion and uncertainty that John felt bewildered, and even a bit fearful of a future in which he had no foil to hate, yet still hated her.

His situation was like that of a bird that has been confined to a cage all of its life, then suddenly the door is opened and it is given full freedom to fly. A decision must be made to either have the courage to go, or to retain the security of the cage and withdraw from the open door. John had to make a choice between throwing off his stepmother's hold over him, or continue to feel shy, withdrawn, lacking in self-esteem, and oppressed by a gut fear of all people.

All through his childhood he had come to view Mary as the prototypical woman, a mean-spirited and cunning sorceress to vent his hate on. Yet here and there in his childhood, there had been bright spots of loving relationships with people who touched him and produced their contrary witness to the potential for nurturing and beneficent human relations. There was Mrs. Storms, his grammar school teacher, who seemed to love every child, or the neighbor Mrs. Crane, who in his childhood had been so loving and kind. Mary's sudden death was very confusing to John's state of mind calling up soul-searching questions.

Dan and John made a last trip to Medford again to view the body of Mary where it was held in a mortuary chapel. They stayed for perhaps a quarter of an hour, both of them in silence, each lost in his own thoughts, and then they left and returned to Sardine Creek. They never attended a funeral for her. If there was a last rite of any kind, it was performed by strangers for a stranger.

So ended the life of Mary White Macdonald. Even her exact age was unknown to John. Probably she was about sixty-seven when she died. Cause of death? Indirectly it was caused by gluttonous eating of bacon grease, bringing on a gall-bladder attack, but also indirectly it was caused by the pet dog, Spot, stealing and bringing back to the cabin on Sardine Creek her proud contribution to the larder, a massive slab of bacon. The dog's contribution was almost a spiritual overlay to the event, as John saw it.

12

After Mary died, Dan's relationship with his son began to change inasmuch as John was the only one left in the family for him to talk to. Dave was living in Milwaukee, Wisconsin, and working for his grandfather Campbell. While there he joined the national guard to help sustain himself. Ron was bumming up and down the West Coast states, finding food and shelter by any means he could. The depression was getting deeper and more intractable as time went on. Eventually, Ron joined the army as means of sustenance.

So Dan tried to reopen a relationship with John by talking to him, and I use the phrase, "talk to," because by this time John had become so constrained by isolation that he could no longer talk "with" his father. He had become so shy that he had lost his ability to carry on a conversation. By now it must have become clear to Dan that his son's education had been seriously neglected. One day it evidently occurred to Dan that John had no sexual education of any kind. From John's perspective, the only thing he knew about sex at age fourteen, had long ago been acquired during his forgotten association with schoolboys during his prepuberty age, telling each other erotic stories and speculating about sex. John had no idea how children were born, no knowledge of the sexual function of women, had never heard of a menstrual cycle. From observation of animals, he had some idea about copulation and was aware of his own erotic arousal when viewing women, but he was almost as ignorant about sex as would be a child of seven or eight years.

Into this void Dan stepped forthrightly to impart to his son the facts of life. He had John sit down with him for a long-delayed father to son chit-chat.

"I would like you to notice the very great difference between males and females," he began. "You can obviously see that all males are superior to females. Notice that the rooster is larger and far more handsome than the hen, and take cattle as an example; notice that the bull is much more handsome and virile compared with the cow. Among people it is obvious that the man is more intelligent and has a better physique than the woman."

John, by this time, was overwhelmed by the sudden beaming attention that his father was bestowing upon him, and so rarely did such an event occur that it was like too high a voltage surge that triggers an electric breaker—he broke into tears. John had no idea why he was crying except that he always cried when people were kind to him. Kindness in his life experience was so unusual that it was emotionally overwhelming. He had always tried to evade these emotional breakthroughs by avoiding socialization. Because of this constriction, his father's sudden attention actually became a barrier to further communication between them. It was too much and too fast. The adjustment to each other would have to be made slowly over years of time. Dan's good intentions were quickly discouraged, and he must have been mystified and frustrated by John's reaction. Fortunately, the sex education that Dan expounded, the inferiority of females, did not become engrafted in John's mind. The sex education lesson just died on the vine.

In this topsy-turvy world view John had evolved, he now felt far more comfortable in being ignored by people, and he was even gratified if they were disparaging, for that confirmed his internal inclination for self-flagellation, and added to the urge to slink away and hide whenever he was subjected to a need to socialize—even with his own father. It would take years of self-therapy to reverse these distortions of his childhood, so deep were the grooves of inversion of normal behavior, so lasting was the influence of his stepmother even long after she was in her grave.

Because of John's warped mental set, Dan's newly established communication with his son settled down to no more than a friendly daily exchange of small talk with no depth, and as he had done in the past with all of his children, he used John, without ever being aware of it, to fulfill his own interests and needs. For example, Dan was an inveterate lifetime smoker. Even when there was no money for food, he would still buy tobacco. On those occasions now when Dan ran out of tobacco, he would give John a nickel and have him walk to Gold Hill, a twenty-four-mile round trip, for a package of Bull Durham smoking tobacco. It never occurred to Dan that it was an unreasonable demand, nor did it occur to John to rebel. Acceding willingly, and by long-established habit, to his father's thoughtlessness of using him like a servant made it unnecessary for John to examine the idea that normal people would be kind enough to each other to exclude such preposterous demands.

Aggravating John's self-image, and adding to his shyness, was the fact that he had not had any new clothing since leaving Michigan years before, and all of his garments were worn out and too small, for he had been growing throughout these years. His hair had become long and unkempt, and he lacked a toothbrush for oral hygiene. His front teeth had all become decayed and infected and were causing a health problem compounded by malnutrition. He was constantly haunted now by a death wish. His only tenuous social connection to other people during these trying times was the Jackson County (rural branch) Library and reading book after book. The vicarious world of literature was his single bridge to normalcy. But his personal life experience was so estranged from what he read of the world that he had to keep the two models of reality separated, as a shadow is separated from the body causing it. His reality was schizoid. Also reading is a practice apt to be done in privacy, and so even this weak link to the human community was compounding the tendency to withdraw.

One day, in the summer of 1932, an old gold prospector leading a little gray burro, came wandering up Sardine Creek past the Macdonalds' cabin. He was a little short wiry man with a stubble of a beard and obviously as tough as his burro, but very friendly. He stopped to chat with Dan and introduced himself as Mr. Sutten. He was one of those lifelong itinerant miners who perpetually roam the earth, all alone and self-dependent. On the burro's back was everything he needed: food, bed roll, tent, gold pan, and tools.

Dan became very interested in Mr. Sutten for the wide spectrum of knowledge the man had about every aspect of gold mining. Sutten explained that he was prospecting for what he called "pocket gold." This was gold that through expulsion to the earth's surface has been freed from an outcropping quartz rock vein, and then after thousands of years of erosional movement, bits of the metal work their way downward from the outcropping in an alluvial fan. By patiently gold-panning in the area, the prospector may gradually trace the gold back to its source, or what Sutten called a pocket. Mr. Sutten graphically told Dan stories about various pockets of gold he had found through the years.

After these rather prolonged conversations, Mr. Sutten left the Macdonalds' cabin to set up camp at the headwaters of Sardine Creek. Then from time to time, the miner and his patient little gray burro would come down from his mountain retreat for supplies and invariably stop by to chat with Dan again. Sutten was obviously a lover of nature, for he told of how he gradually was enticing a little doe deer to come to his campsite each day to be fed potato peelings, and he liked to recount other animal and nature stories. One got the impression that the man was using the excuse of mining gold to justify a meandering life of enjoying the wilderness. But Dan was not moved by stories about nature, and he made it known that his interest was in being able to mine gold on a large enough scale to make it pay. Mr. Sutten casually remarked that he had the equipment to do just that, but it didn't interest him.

Dan's attention was turned on like a light bulb.

"Well, what does your equipment consist of?" Dan asked.

Sutten explained that there was about five hundred feet of piping of heavy-gauge sheet metal pipeline, starting at sixteen-inch diameter stuff, and gradually tapering down to four-inch diameter, and there was a hydraulic gun weighing about a half ton or more, with various sizes and types of nozzles, and assorted other pieces of equipment, all of it stored on a lot he owned in Medford. Dan was very quiet for a moment, and then he asked very casually what he would sell it for. Sutten guessed it would be worth about five hundred dollars. Dan, of course, did not have five hundred cents, but that did not produce the slightest discouragement. Dan could smell a deal, and he quickly suggested that Mr. Sutten should stay for supper.

Dan's cooking skills were abominable. His cuisine ran to potatoes fried in lots of grease and black with pepper, together with blood rare hunks of meat. Green and yellow vegetables he dismissed as inappropriate to a good meal. But if Mr. Sutten was unimpressed by the food, he was too gracious to indicate it. Throughout the evening he and Dan talked about hydraulic placer mining. During the following days, Mr. Sutten was invited to dinner quite often, even though Dan and John's food rations were quite limited at the time. Mr. Sutten politely accepted all the invitations, even though he must have become, by that time, fully aware that Dan's cooking was a bilious abomination.

For about two weeks, off and on, they haggled before they struck a deal. Since the hydraulic mining equipment was just sitting on a vacant lot in Medford, Dan and John would bring it up Sardine Creek, and set it all up as a demonstration exhibit, so that Sutten could sell it easily. While they were waiting for an interested purchaser to show up, Dan and John would use the equipment for their own placer mining and Mr. Sutten would be paid ten percent of the profit from their earnings. There was no formal contract—just a verbal agreement that they shook hands to ratify. Dan's deal was a little bit like an iceberg, much of it was invisible below the dark water. Once he got the mining equipment set up and operating, he explained to John, the finding of a prospective buyer could endure for unending time. Besides, the mining operation on Sardine Creek would be so far back in the wilderness that the risk of finding a buyer was almost nil, and anyway who was there in 1932 who had five hundred dollars? Dan was very pleased with himself. It was his first real business adventure since leaving Michigan years ago.

About a year before Dan's deal was made, two prospectors had come up Sardine Creek and wandered up a side arroyo called Gold Gulch. The gulch was downstream from the Macdonalds' cabin about two miles. The prospectors started working almost at the crown of the gulch, and were digging holes down to bedrock and panning the gravel scraped out of the rock cavities. They were not finding anything.

But one day as they were walking past a pile of topsoil that they had dug up, one of the men saw a glitter. The miner picked up the object and was astonished to find it was a nugget of gold about three quarters of an inch across and an eighth of an inch thick. It had obviously been lying right on the surface of the ground. The nugget generated a good deal of speculation about Gold Gulch. Because the nugget was on the surface, the conjecture was that it could have been carried there by an early prospector who may have just lost it there.

Dan had seen the nugget and heard the story, so when Mr. Sutten came along with his hydraulic mining equipment, Dan decided unequivocally that the downstream mouth of Gold Gulch was the ideal place to do his mining, even though there were quite a number of negative realities he should have considered: First, the land was privately owned and Dan had no permission to mine there. Second, the large nugget that had been found in the gulch was not native to the area. Third, to get water for the operation, it would be necessary to build a dam to divert water out of Sardine Creek and that would require a permit from the state. Fourth, even at that time, the state of Oregon was frowning on hydraulic mining for the way it scarred the land. Dan simply did not dwell on any of this.

Just as soon as he could, Dan cranked up the old Nash, hitched on the trailer, and headed for Medford to fetch the hydraulic mining equipment.

The piping was heavy and bulky, and the car and trailer could only carry limited loads up the steep mountain road to the depot as near to Gold Gulch as Dan could get, actually about a half mile away from the mining site. Over a period of a week or more, he managed to get it all transported from Medford.

The next part of the job was for Dan and John to carry all the pipe, piece by piece, on their shoulders, the half-mile to the mining area. With that done they had to find a way to haul in the heavy hydraulic gun, which weighed over a half ton. Moving it presented a considerable challenge to one man and a teenager. To accomplish this Dan cut down small trees, squared them into timbers with an adze, and bolted the timbers together to form a crude sled on which the gun was mounted.

When the sled was finished, Dan hooked onto it with a compound block-and-tackle set, fastened the other end of his pulley assembly to a convenient tree, and he and John pulled and dragged the sled along for about twenty feet till the massive iron gun was up to the anchor tree. At that point Dan found another anchor tree, hooked on his block-and-tackle again, and dragged it another twenty feet, and in these repeated cycles of finding anchor trees and dragging the gun, they worked their way toward getting it a half mile up Gold Gulch to the mining site. The job required several weeks of strenuous effort before all of the equipment was assembled on the site. John found that his reading days were over. There was no more time to make a weekly hike to the county library.

The next part of the project was to determine how to get a large enough volume of water high on the side of the arroyo, several hundred feet directly above the mining site, to provide the hydraulic water pressure to satisfactorily operate the gun down in the bottom of Gold Gulch. Sardine Creek was a fast-running stream, and Dan calculated that by going upstream about a mile and diverting water from the creek into a relatively level diversion ditch dug along the contour of the adjacent valley wall, he could just nicely get a flow of feed water up to the required elevation at the mouth of Gold Gulch.

To provide for the diversion water at the selected upstream site on Sardine Creek, Dan and John began the job of building a six-foot-high dam in the creek. To begin the dam construction, Dan selected a good-sized fir tree growing near the creek bank, and they felled it directly across the creek bed. Then they cut a log out of the tree that was just long enough to span the creek width. Next they dug notches down into the soil on each side of the creek and rolled the spanning log down into the notches, which had been dug at just the right places to place the log six feet above the creek bed to form the top of the dam. He and John then cut great numbers of poles, four to six inches in diameter, and banked them against the upstream side of the spanning log. The poles were covered with fir boughs and then the entire structure covered with earth. In the summer season, there was very little water flowing in the creek, so they carried the whole stream away in a tunnel under the dam while it was being constructed.

At the top of the dam, they built a wooden overflow structure to carry away the excess water, if it rose too high to be contained. Even though the dam leaked some, it held back enough water for their needs during the winter high-water season, and that would be the only time in which there would be enough water for hydraulic mining anyway.

From the site of this newly completed dam and water source, Dan now began to plan a transport ditch to carry the water all the way to the hydraulic mining site, a distance of just about one mile. The ditch had to follow a very careful gradient or fall, so the water would flow slowly and uniformly for the entire distance while gaining the required elevation of about four hundred feet at the terminal end. To measure the proper gradient, it would be necessary to construct a crude surveying tool to use while digging the ditch.

Dan selected a nice straight ten-foot piece of lumber, and nailed a three-cornered tripod to the center of the instrument board from which he suspended a plumb bob. With the instrument board set exactly one inch lower at one end than at the other, Dan marked exactly where the plumb bob pointed at the center of his board, to indicate one inch of incline for each ten linear feet of ditching. By using this crude instrument, he would measure the proper gradient for the entire one mile of ditch as it was being dug.

Dan calculated that the ditch would need to be eighteen inches deep, a foot wide at the bottom, and eighteen inches wide at the top. The tapered walls were to prevent soil from sloughing down off the sides, and caving into the ditch when the soil was saturated with water. The entire ditch would be dug by hand, with pick and shovel, through a dense virgin forest and along the steep side of the mountain. John was appalled by the enormity of the project for just two people, but Dan didn't seem to think that the job was anything extraordinary. John just complied with the plan in silence, for at that time he never questioned anything his father proposed.

They began the ditch-digging in the summer of 1933. It was President Roosevelt's first year in office, and a period of brief optimism in which the people were hoping that somehow the new president could lead the nation out of the depths of the depression that had now grown worldwide. But none of the exciting political news was heard by Dan and John, isolated as they were and preoccupied by Dan's single-minded vision. They soon fell into a monotonous routine from early morning to late evenings, digging their water supply ditch around trees and through rock outcroppings, one inch of decline to each ten feet of ditching, skirting the bottom slope of the mountainside adjacent to Sardine Creek. It was a boring and exhausting expenditure of energy.

After a month or so of this strenuous activity, Dan began to grow tired of the job. He would come to work in the morning and put in a few hours of work, then leave and go back to the cabin for the rest of the day, leaving John to work by himself. Dan's assumption was that John was younger and therefore strong enough to put in a full day's work, while he, because of his age, should be excused from that much effort. Dan dismissed from his mind that John was carrying on this back-breaking labor at age fifteen, and without adequate food.

But regardless of the futility of the job and in spite of the arduous labor required to do it, John acquiesced fully with his father's wishes because he had been taught by the overt discipline during his childhood that compliance was his solemn duty. His father never intimidated John, and there was no threat of reprisal if he didn't do the work, but there didn't need to be because Mary's influence had long ago conditioned him to comply without question to whatever his father required of him.

Sometimes the hunger was overpowering. When that happened John would leave the ditch-digging and hike to the top of Gold Gulch where the two prospectors, who had found the original nugget that had inspired Dan's mining plan, were still encamped. John knew from previous sorties to their camp, while they were gone, that they had a fifty-pound sack of dried prunes in their tent.

John would carefully check out where the men were working, and then steal into the tent and snatch up a pocket full of prunes, with the hope that the miners would not become aware of the loss. Each theft was an act of desperation that frightened him. They were a couple of tough prospectors, and it is possible they would have shot him had they ever caught him in the act.

Dan and John worked on the ditch about six months and at last after what seemed like endless time, it was finished. In the meantime Mr. Sutten had given up mining on Sardine Creek, and had departed to seek his fortune elsewhere. He did not leave a forwarding address and that gave Dan a carte blanche sense of freedom to use Mr. Sutten's equipment any way he desired.

The next phase of the mining plan could now begin: building sluice boxes. For this Dan needed lumber, lots of it, to construct about a hundred feet or more of the large troughlike wooden sluices with their accompanying riffles, and they would also need a large wooden receiving tank for the feed water to pour into at the terminal end of their water supply ditch. In the receiving tank, a junction was to be made to the pipeline that would carry water down to the hydraulic gun. Dan had no money to buy lumber with for the construction of the wooden components, but given his eternal optimism and inventive mind, together with a bit of perfidy, a lack of lumber was just one more minor detail to find a solution to.

About two miles above the Gold Gulch mining site was the homestead land and house that Dan had come to Sardine Creek to occupy, but had never moved into because it was too far away from the logging trail by which they drove back and forth to town. Dan asserted to John, "The house is just standing there vacant. We may as well use it. It will make an excellent source of seasoned lumber." The fact that the house and land had been reclaimed for taxes by the county produced no significant impression on Dan's single-minded preoccupation with his mining plans. The house was a good inhabitable building and had never been vandalized because of its remoteness—almost at the top of a mountain pass. The lumber and material used in its construction must have been brought there by mule pack train sometime during the eighteen hundreds. All of the flooring and ceiling joists were made of knot-free straight grained ponderosa pine.

"Ideal for sluice boxes," Dan asserted.

They began the job of dismantling the entire two-bedroom house, board by board. They pulled all the nails and straightened them very carefully to be used later, and took down all the siding. The lap siding was beautiful aromatic cedar that had never been painted. Lumber of that quality is no longer available anywhere. It took a couple of months to dismantle the house and salvage all the lumber, and then the next project was to get it down the mountain two miles to the mining site. Since there was no road, the only way to get it there was to pack all of it on their backs, and so piece by piece, the entire two-bedroom house was carried down to Gold Gulch.

By the time the carpentry was finished in 1933, the summer was ebbing to autumn. It had taken them well over a year to complete the herculean job of setting up all the equipment for hydraulic mining, and John at age fifteen had done most of the work under his father's direction and supervision. All that remained now was for the oncoming winter to produce enough water to carry out Dan's plan, and then triumphantly, with whatever remaining submission and loyalty he could get from his children, he would try to gather them all together again at Sardine Creek to mine gold, so that once more he would regain his position as the paternal head of the family, for that had been the ultimate purpose of the entire project. Early American history was grounded in a patriarchal father who directed his large family, as a cooperative enterprise to carry on the work of the mostly rural farm life, and Dan had not yet given up this role that he deemed was his right and his responsibility.

13

Dan sent letters out to brothers Dave and Ron. Ron had left the army and was working at picking fruit in Southern California, and Dave was working for his grandfather in Milwaukee, Wisconsin. The fruit season was over, so Ron returned as soon as he got his letter. He caught a ride on a freight train and got off in Gold Hill, from which he would have to hike in to the Macdonald cabin on Sardine Creek. He decided to take a cross-country shortcut over the mountains. He started out late in the afternoon and was caught by darkness of night high up on a mountain pass.

It was a bitter cold night, so he made a fire to sleep by through the night. Ron was wearing a heavy sheepskin coat and all night he kept backing up to the fire as he slept, to keep warm. He awoke during the night to some discomfort on his backside and discovered to his chagrin that his coat was afire. He shed the garment hastily and beat out the flames, but it had already burned a large hole in the back of the coat. Assessing the situation he decided the coat was too valuable to throw away. Where would he ever get another sheepskin coat, given his impoverished situation? So he appeared next day at the cabin on Sardine Creek, unkempt from traveling and sleeping out, and with a gaping burned hole in his coat.

Brother Dave's return to Sardine Creek was more circuitous. About the time that Dan was writing his letter to his sons to come home for the hydraulic mining project, Sister Helen was quitting her job in Florida to return home to Montague, Michigan, where she had friends from childhood whom she wanted to visit.

It was a nostalgic village for her, and she had a longing to return and visit her old friends. During the return visit, she became acquainted with a young man named Scotty Perkins, from the neighboring town of Whitehall. He was a colorful and handsome lad, somewhat younger than she, with a talent for folk music that was a source of popularity wherever he went. Helen had never been seriously courted before, and before she knew what had happened, they were engaged.

Helen wrote to her brother Dave, in Milwaukee, about her planned marriage. Her husband, she assured him, could readily earn money by performing folk music, and she would try to find a new job of some kind. Dave wrote back to his sister, and her new husband, about their father's letter that he had just received, pleading for them to come to Oregon and the cabin on Sardine Creek. Dan was sure they could make a good living at hydraulic gold mining. "Gold" is an enrapturing word—they made an immediate decision to pool their limited money, buy a car, and all drive back to Oregon together. They shopped around and found an old Chevrolet for sale for thirty dollars that was in reasonably good running order, even if the tires were in bad shape. In their Chevrolet they would become latter-day argonauts in search of the golden fleece.

The only ties that Dave and Helen still had in Montague were the family possessions that had been left in storage in a relative's barn, when the family had migrated West in 1929.

They went to the storage barn to sort through furniture, dishes, and knickknacks, for a few things to take West with them. Helen selected some family pictures, a silver tea set that had been a wedding gift at their father and mother's wedding, a very old sword that had belonged to Dan's stepfather and was prized by their father, and a cut glass pitcher that Dan had given his foster mother when he was a child. With these few remedial belongings from the Macdonalds' farm, they set out together for Oregon in late autumn of 1933.

It was a trip beset with troubles. They ran out of money about half way across the United States, and in desperation took the silver tea set to a pawn shop. The shop owner immediately assumed it was stolen property and treated them as criminals. The tea set was a finely engraved pure silver antique that had never been used, but the pawn shop owner would only give them a pittance. They were forced to sadly sacrifice the family heirloom, and with the money bought gasoline at ten cents a gallon to get on their way again.

But now the car tires were giving out. The tires were patched till they could be patched no more. They were traveling through the Great Plains wheat belt states at that time, and that gave Dave an idea for a wheat belt solution to the problem. The gaping holes in the tires were sealed by cutting out sections of discarded junk tires, shaping the sections for patches, and gluing them with rubber cement to bridge the blowout holes. Tires, in those days, required inner tubes that were inflated, but they had no money to buy replacement inner tubes.

They found a source of wheat, and Dave filled the tire casings with as much of the seed as he could. Then they soaked the tires in water to expand the seed to produce enough volume to expand the tires sufficiently to drive on them. With these heavy squishy tubeless tires, they rolled on toward Oregon and eventually made it to Gold Hill.

Dan was elated when they arrived and confided that their troubles were over because as soon as there was enough water in Sardine Creek they would begin hydraulic mining. But there was another immediate problem to solve while they were waiting for the rain; there were now six people to find food for. None of them had either a job or money to live on.

When economic systems fail, people naturally fall back on a barter system of trading, and that was now beginning to occur everywhere in the nation. Dan found a farmer down in Sam's Valley who had an apple orchard in which the apples were just falling off the trees to waste because it didn't pay to have them picked. In the deeply depressed economy, no one had money to buy apples or anything else. Dan arranged for the whole family to pick apples and press them into cider with the farmer's cider press. Somewhere, Dan found eight wooden barrels to fill with cider, and the arrangement was that the farmer would get four barrels of cider, and Dan would get the other four barrels. Cider is a delicious drink, but it hardly makes up for meat and vegetables, so now Dan found another farmer who would swap cider for onions. So they acquired several hundred pounds of onions.

The swapping arrangements could have gone on to work out a more varied menu, but by that time, the winter rains were starting and so Dan curtailed the exchanges, narrowing the food variety to just onions and cider. Brother Ron began filling in by hunting for any creature he could find to shoot. He came in one day with a baby goat that he had mistaken for a fawn deer. They cooked onions in every varied way they could imagine, but however they were cooked, the singleness of their vegetable source began to pall. The barrels of cider fermented just a bit to give it a nice tingle to the tongue and was delicious.

When Sardine Creek began filling to its embankments,

the dam that Dan and John had constructed filled with water nicely. They opened the water supply gate into their mile-long transmission ditch. The flow rate was just right, and water passed through it properly just as had been planned. At Gold Gulch, the receiving tank filled and flowed into the piping system to build a great pressure for operating the hydraulic gun. The whole system was an unqualified success, and there was a feeling of optimism and jubilation in the family buoyed by the fact that they were enjoying a full family reunion after years of separation.

Dan divided the family into two crews, one to work days, the other nights. Dan was jubilant—he was in control of his family again. The night crew built great bonfires to illuminate the workings. It was all very exciting to direct the water stream with its enormous pressure at boulders and over-burden and watch it just melt away.

Boulders as large as a bucket could be driven about like pebbles. Gravel swished down through the sluice boxes in an endless stream. The engineering part of the project, which Dan had supervised, was highly successful. In minutes they could sluice out tons of gravel, which by laborious pick and shovel hand work would take hours and days to accomplish. But then! When they cleaned their riffles out, there was no gold in them. They continued to work the mine for about three weeks, obtaining only trace amounts of gold. It became very clear that there was not enough gold in the area to justify further mining. The water was shut off and the whole project abandoned. For John, at age fifteen, about two full years of his life had been wasted in isolation, hunger, and hard labor.

Dan, too, was beaten. He never tried gold mining again, and indeed he rarely ever discussed gold mining again. It was also the last time that he was ever permitted to patriarchically direct the family.

It was now necessary to find some way to feed the family through the winter months of 1934. The following summer the boys could anticipate working again in the California fruit orchards, but for the time being, Dan's failed gold mine had left them destitute. There was by now some scattered federal government relief efforts, such as the Civilian Conservation Corps, commonly known by the acronym "CCC." But it was too limited and unavailable to help them any. The nation's populace was in an angry mood.

President Roosevelt was trying desperately to respond by experimenting with a bevy of new and novel ideas to stimulate the economy, but by now the depression had become so intractable and so worldwide that to produce any movement toward freeing it was futile. His efforts were like trying to move an enormously heavy freight train by merely putting his shoulder to the job. What was needed was the power of a behemoth economic engine of some kind.

The Macdonald family, a typical micro unit in this macro global tragedy, cast about trying to find some way to at least obtain food to sustain themselves till spring came, with perhaps the hope of finding agricultural work by then. Down the creek several miles from the Macdonalds' cabin, there was a family named Ritter, and they had firewood cutting rights to the timber there. Dave and Ron struck a deal with the Ritters to cut firewood during the remainder of the winter. They were not to be paid any money, but they would be credited with three dollars a cord, in food only, from a local grocery store. The whole family went to work with zeal felling trees, and cutting and splitting them into cords of firewood.

The family had to cut wood in advance of getting any

groceries, so there was an interim time when all they had to eat was onions and cider, and an illegally poached deer Ron managed to shoot. All wood-cutting at that time was done by hand with two-man cross-cut saws and axes. The chain saw and hydraulic splitter were not yet invented.

The work was the hardest kind of manual labor, but made even harder to endure by their limited food supply, and also the winter's snow was accumulating.

After a week or two of initial start-up time, they had produced enough cords of firewood to trade for groceries. That first load of foodstuff was like Thanksgiving day; the whole family joined together in a holiday festivity. Sister Helen cooked gigantic meals of homemade bread, vegetables, meats, and pastries. With the first breakfast served, after the family obtained food, Dave ate twenty-four good sized pancakes smothered in butter and jam, and John consumed eighteen. Although the work was hard, there was a family spirit again to their enterprise, and a happy enjoyment of the reunion after so many years of separation. In spite of the failure of the gold mine, it was the best winter they had since coming West in 1929. They had no money, but they were not hungry, and they had each other, and at the time, that was even better than money.

When spring came Dave and Ron left the wood-cutting and hopped a freight train heading for California and the fruit orchards. Sister Helen and her new husband headed out to Klamath Falls, Oregon, where there was said to be work available in the lumber mills. Dan and John were once again left to their own devices at the cabin on Sardine Creek. Dan gave up wood-cutting as soon as the rest of the family left. He was not inclined to carry on such heavy work if an easier way of making a living could be found.

Dan found a job in Sam's Valley for both he and John, working at odds and ends for food only, at a turkey farm.

John herded turkeys astride a gentle old horse that knew how to do it even better than the rider. The idea was to graze the birds by slowly urging them to move to new grounds. They lived there in reasonable comfort for a time during which there was evidently an exchange of letters between Dan and his sons in California, in which an arrangement plan was made concerning John. One day brother Dave surprisingly appeared at the cabin on Sardine Creek and informed John that he would take him south to get a job on an apricot ranch near Davis, California, where he and Ron were working. John was very pleased to get away from Sardine Creek where he had been living in isolation with his father for so many years that it had devastated his personality and ruined his chance of getting a public school education.

The two brothers rolled up what few clothes John had, secured them inside of a sleeping blanket, and set off on foot for Gold Hill. There they waited patiently for a freight train to be made up on a rail siding. Dave found an oil tanker car, which has a small platform at each end of the car where a couple of men can conveniently hitch a ride. They got aboard and by early morning, their engineer blasted a few hoots at the street crossings as they slowly rolled out of Gold Hill heading for California.

For John it was a heady experience to travel away from home and become one of the thousands of transient men and some women who were wandering about all over the nation, usually by this same mode of travel that they were using. To accommodate the hordes of drifters, almost every sizable town had begun setting up shelters, usually run by the Salvation Army, where a man could find a bunk to sleep in and a free meal, and sometimes even a shower. It was an interesting time in which, with all the privation, there was really very little crime, and one could travel from one end of the nation to the other with little fear of molestation.

The freight train was pulled by what was called a reverse malley, featuring a steam-driven engine in which the engineer's cab was out front ahead of the steam boiler. It was a powerful and enormously heavy brute of a machine designed for mountain climbing. The train slowly wended its way up over the Siskiyou Mountain Range past a glorious snow-covered Mount Shasta, on through the town of Dunsmuir, and down into the San Joaquin Valley. It was a pleasant experience for John listening to the click-click of the rail ends, the rhythmic chugging of the massive steam pistons, and the long mournful blasts of the steam whistle at road crossings. As they moved south, there was an accompanying feeling of a change of climate as well as a change of scenery from the lush Oregon timber lands to the California green acres of fruit crops and hay fields, and all the small farm towns of the Central Valley.

Dave and John disembarked from their oil tanker freight car in Sacramento, where Dave phoned brother Ron to come and pick them up with the ranch's pickup truck. The three boys, happy to be reunited, drove back to the apricot ranch near Davis, California. The ranch was owned by a Mr. Thurber, a kindly old gentleman with fatherly warmth. The apricot trees were sagging with luscious pastel fruit. John found that he had already been assigned a bed in a clean neat bunkhouse. Fruit picking was just starting.

For the first time in his life, John began to earn money that was his, and for the first time since leaving Michigan years ago, he was able to buy clothing, get a haircut by a barber, eat the food of his choice, and enjoy all the freedoms of choice that most people take for granted. It was like being released from prison to be away from Sardine Creek and all the privations of his teen years. He had a wonderful summer of joy being with his brothers. But joy can only be measured in relative values, and his joy was relative to his bleak past, for actually he was only earning a few pennies per hour, but the circumstances of freedom were nevertheless utopian for him at the time.

When the apricot season was over and the job ended, John bought a bus ticket to return to Gold Hill and the cabin on Sardine Creek. There he found Dan as he had left him some months before but changed in attitude. Dan was overjoyed to see his youngest son again.

14

There seemed to be a new camaraderie between them, and John felt he had gained some new esteem from his father by his three months of absence. There were a number of new things that had occurred during that summer that they could talk about.

First, while John was away, Dan had bartered away the entire hydraulic mining assembly, in spite of the fact that it was owned by Mr. Sutten, who had disappeared from the scene. Somehow it had escaped Dan's mind that the hydraulic outfit was not his to sell. All of the stuff was traded to the Smith cattle ranch folks for two one-hundred pound sacks of dried beans, and of all things, a bushel of dried peaches. So when John returned to Sardine Creek, he found his father's food rations to consist largely of beans and peaches—sometimes cooked together, for Dan wasn't very discriminatory about cooking food, and anyway it was a change from the cider and onions of the winter before.

But during the summer, Dan had also had a stroke of luck. The boys had shipped home from Southern California a box of old winter work clothing. The clothes were almost worthless, but for some unknown reason, they had insured them for a hundred dollars. While the package was in the express office, a thief broke in to rob the safe. He used the package of clothing to muffle the sound and contain the dynamite charge to blow the safe. The clothing was shredded, and Dan was delighted. Wringing his hands with pleasure, he collected the full insurance.

The one hundred dollars was more than adequate to keep Dan in Bull Durham smoking tobacco and a supply of meat to cook with his beans for the entire summer, and there was even money left over.

Another development that had occurred during the summer was a rumor Dan heard that people now could get employment picking hops near the neighboring town of Grant's Pass, a few miles distant. The Eighteenth Amendment to the Constitution had been repealed, making alcoholic beverages legal again, so the growing of hops to make beer was becoming a profitable new farm crop. The anticipation of a renewed liquor industry also began arousing latent memories in Dan's mind about the time, long ago in Michigan, when he had experimented with setting up his own still in the cellar of the house to produce brandy from fermented and discarded canned fruit.

"Before we go to Grant's Pass to pick hops, I'm going to try to do something interesting with these leftover dried peaches," Dan confided to John. He took the twenty pounds or so of peaches and dumped them into an empty cider barrel, tossed in ten pounds of sugar, and filled the barrel half full of water. Then they cranked up the old Nash and headed north.

Work was readily available, but it was a miserable job. The owners were clearly exploiting the poor ragged workers who had not had jobs for years past and were in desperate circumstances.

The workers were paid in scrip instead of money, and the scrip could only be used at a company store, at which food and supplies of extremely poor quality and excessively high prices were to be purchased with it. Only limited amounts of scrip, left over after the family had bought supplies, could be exchanged for real money. Field privies were never cleaned and became intolerable, there were no showers, and no safe water supply was provided employees. Drinking water was dipped from irrigation ditches. Very quickly the entire encampment of workers was ravaged by dysentery. Sick babies and children could be heard crying all through the nights. An ugly tension settled over the encampment, and each night Communist spokesmen would gather crowds of workers around a bonfire and discuss revolution. It was clear to Dan that riots could break out at any time in that tense atmosphere, so he and John only worked long enough to get the means to return to the peaceful wilds of Sardine Creek.

Back at the cabin, Dan found his dried peach brew bubbling and raising a gratifying scum to the surface of the fluid. He cleared away enough of the sudsy foam to dip out a glass of the fermenting juice. Dan took a long draft of the evil-looking fluid and smacked his lips. Flinging the foam from his mustache, he burped a satisfying release and commented that "It was a little green," meaning that the brew needed more aging, but his eyes lit up in anticipation. At an invitation from his father, John dipped into the barrel for a glass of the suds too, and found it rather hostile to his taste buds.

John didn't want to mar their new relationship by showing derision for the concoction, so he gulped and swallowed it with reluctance. The two of them each tried another glass in a spirit of camaraderie—and then another glass.

As time passed, the world seemed to John to have altered. The distorted lines of gravity from the "House of Mystery" on the north fork of Sardine Creek somehow had drifted to their cabin on the south fork. It also suddenly occurred to John that when he got back from Grant's Pass, he had seen fresh deer tracks at the cattle salt-lick near their cabin. Evening was now approaching and an inebriated idea floated through his mind; he would shoot a deer for the larder. He bound a flashlight to the barrel of the old Remington rifle that Brother Ron had so many times used to tip the balance between starvation and meat for the table, and John made his way to the salt-lick.

After some frantic scrambling, he managed to climb up a neighboring madrone tree within sight of the salt-lick, and he hid himself there to wait for the deer. By this time he was salivating for venison. Shortly after dark, a nice fat doe came down out of the forest to the salt-lick. John turned on the flashlight that was attached to the rifle barrel and directed the light at the animal. Unfortunately it was the kind of beam that spreads instead of focusing a spot of light, so it didn't help much as a means of aiming the gun. John aimed as best he could and squeezed off a shot.

Nothing happened; the deer just stood there in plain sight. He shot again and again. The doe just stood entranced and immobilized by the bright light. After a while it became clear to John that he was spraying the bushes with an awful lot of bullets. The deer seemed to have an invincible shield about her, or perhaps the peach cordial and the altered lines of gravity from the "House of Mystery" were interfering. At any rate the fat little doe just continued to stand there in the light of the flashlight, seemingly in a hypnotic trance, or perhaps there was a more shameful explanation; she was just too scornful to move, given the inaccuracy of the spray of bullets around her.

By now John had shot away all the cartridges in the gun, but he was determined not to give up. Carefully holding the flashlight trained on the animal, he climbed down from the tree and cautiously approached closer, and then even closer, and then he walked up to her, shining the flashlight into her eyes, and still she did not bolt. Having exhausted any other means of killing the deer, he made a final decision to club her with the rifle. But alas the peach juice was still altering his faculties and he missed. The blow struck over the back of her neck. Evidently it was a good substantial swing, for the stock broke off of the rifle and John tossed the worthless barrel away with disgust.

But now suddenly the doe awoke from her trance and did begin to bolt. At this point John became stubborn. He was not going to be outwitted now, so he grabbed frantically onto her tail.

The indignity of this stupid boy pulling her tail was just too much. The doe now put her full energy to work, fleeing into a tangled grove of manzanita brush. John, determined not to be defeated, clung with tenacity to the tail and was yanked headlong through the bushes at top speed, with ripping clothing, tearing scratches, and bloody abrasions. At last the exhausted animal, with John still in tow hanging on to her tail, leaped from an embankment down into Sardine Creek where she collapsed. John triumphantly sat on her for a few minutes in the middle of the creek to collect his faculties and make a decision as to what to do now at this climactic moment of his first successful deer hunt.

Obviously the animal was dead, but she had certainly put up a magnificent battle. How he could brag to his brother Ron about this. No need to tell how this strange hunt had been conducted. What was important was that he had bagged a deer. John got up off the dead carcass to consider how he would drag his trophy home. But suddenly, revived by the cold water, the deer was very much alive again. She scrambled to her feet and in great energetic bounds sped away into the forest, flicking her white tail derisively.

With hang-dog shame, John wearily trudged back to the cabin, soaking wet from the creek, his clothing torn to ribbons, and bleeding from innumerable scratches and abrasions. It was the last time he would ever hunt. The rifle was ruined, and so was his reputation as a hunter. He felt immensely sorry for the deer, too.

The poor animal had suffered such indignity as well as a bruised neck. The whole episode was such a total disaster that John determined that he would just try to forget that it had ever happened.

The following day Mr. King, their once hostile neighbor, happened by. Dan, with great enthusiasm, introduced King to the half-barrel of fermenting peach juice. They hadn't been on speaking terms for several years before when Mr. King had threatened to shoot any of the Macdonalds caught stealing his apples. The peach cordial quickly appeased any awkward feeling between them. The two men settled down in chairs next to the grog and were soon reconciled as old buddies, exchanging long stories of mining adventures and gold-glittering wealth, with each dipping from time to time into the barrel of bubbling brew. Eventually each of them drifted from alcoholic soliloquies to alcoholic somnolence, and they both slept peacefully beside their barrel.

Dan had not had a drink of anything alcoholic since leaving Michigan years before, and the renewed experience jarred awake his long latent craving for the mind-altering affect. He was not a man who dealt easily with the harshness of reality. Alcohol since early youth had been the catalyst to alter his mind for viewing life in a romantic aura so he could tolerate the jagged edges of it.

The next day the two men continued in their jovial fellowship, each dipping into the bubbling brew at ever more frequent intervals till they passed again into somnolent golden dreams of unimaginable bonanzas. John became alarmed by the situation. With an entire half barrel of this poisonous stuff to draw from, where would it end? He had to take some kind of action. He made the most assertive decision regarding his father that he had ever made before. He would just have to risk the anger it would provoke. He dumped the entire barrel of fermenting peach juice.

When Mr. King awoke, his normal flamboyant bristling red beard was matted with scum from the yeasty brew, and his slept-in clothing was all awry. He forlornly stumbled homeward down the Sardine Creek logging trail. Dan spent a couple of sobering days of sick recovery. To John's surprise he was not angry, and in fact he exhibited a rather hang-dog shame about the incident.

Father and son were again left in peace at the isolated cabin with little more to do than observe the little lonely world around the cabin, a microcosm of mountain wilderness and animal life seldom intruded upon by humans. For John, it was interesting to observe the variety of forest animals. He alone was the almost only clumsy predator in the area, for the headwaters of Sardine Creek were just too remote for most hunters.

One of the most interesting animals that were in rather generous numbers around the cabin was porcupines. The front porch of the Macdonalds' cabin had some peculiar attraction for these creatures. Often at night they would come onto the porch and chew the wood flooring. It may have been that there was salt in the lumber, which they craved, or it may have been, as some naturalists assert, that porcupine teeth continue to grow throughout their life and need to be ground down by gnawing. Whatever the cause, the amount of noise their grinding teeth made during the night was very disturbing.

One night John was abruptly awakened to the sounds of overturning furniture and crashing blows. In alarm he leaped to his feet and peered out into the living room of the cabin to witness an amazing sight. Dan was up and wearing a long white nightgown, an article of clothing he still clung to from their more domestic life in Michigan long ago. He was dashing about the room madly in his nighty, with an ax in one hand and a kerosene lamp in the other, taking vicious swings with the ax at a porcupine that was fleeing about the room seeking a way to escape. It seemed that the animal had been gnawing the wood on the front porch so loudly that Dan couldn't sleep. Lighting the lamp and picking up the ax, he opened the door intending to bash the poor animal, but the porcupine had other ideas and bolted into the house.

Dan triumphantly yelled, "Ha!" and slammed the door shut. Then began the frantic pursuit that had awakened John.

In his long white nightgown, holding his lamp aloft, Dan was chasing the animal all about the room while taking great smashing blows, trying to terminate the creature's life. After a furious chase, the ax finally found its mark, and in the following days, father and son enjoyed the delicacy of crushed porcupine stew.

The floor of the Macdonald cabin was somewhat unique in that the flooring had innumerable knotholes in it. Someone in the past had tried to add a bit of esthetic nicety to dress the cabin up by nailing tin-can lids over the knotholes. Evidently the effort had been exhausted by so many holes that the tenant had run out of tin-can lids, so quite a number of open knotholes still remained by which one could look straight down through the holes to the earth beneath the house. One day shortly after the peach juice wine had been imbibed, Dan and John were sitting in the kitchen of their cabin chatting amicably while they ate lunch. In the middle of a sentence, Dan blurted, "And look at that damn snake!" Instead, John looked at his father anxiously. Was this a delayed delirium from the peach brew? But Dan pointed to an open knothole in the floor, and sure enough a small snake was writhing its way up through the floor. Then John wondered if two people could have the same delusion at the same time. He shook his head in disbelief.

One of the hazards of the Sardine Creek valley was the great numbers of rattlesnakes. In a breeding storm one year, they could not leave the cabin without a good stout club to deter snakes, and in that one season alone, they gathered an entire cigar box full of rattles from the snakes they had destroyed. The snakes were often just outside the door of their cabin, and a danger to any small animal as John found out when he tried to raise a few chickens. One day he observed a rattlesnake hypnotizing a half-grown chicken. The snake, weaving its head slowly from side to side with beady eyes fixed on the chicken, was gradually writing its way into ever closer position to strike when John interfered with a stout club.

While John was having almost no social life during the isolated years at the Sardine Creek cabin, he had a compensating relationship with the wilderness that is seldom experienced in the urban world of hustle-bustle. The great beauty of Oregon's ancient virgin forests together with the wildlife habitat, and the clear sparkling star-studded nights, the weather changing seasons of the deep forests, all were trade-offs that altered and enhanced his vision of nature in which he often contemplated about the awesome work of the Creator. He was removed from a social agenda, but that freed him to both observe and feel the mystical.

15

It was now the summer of 1935 and tiny relief cracks were beginning to be visible in the Great Depression. President Roosevelt, through courageous experimentation, had greatly changed and enlarged the social responsibilities of the federal government, but he never really found any substantial means to stimulate the economy. He was, however, able to mitigate much of the privation, and for this he was acclaimed as a great and popular president, especially by the hordes of poor people.

Brothers Dave and Ron had decided to move to San Francisco to try to find work. Dave found a job working for a scale company utilizing the skills he had learned from his Grandfather Campbell in Milwaukee. Brother Ron found odds and ends jobs to keep him afloat till he found a rather good blacksmith job working for the Southern Pacific Rail Company. The two brothers pooled their money and bought a second-hand luxury Auburn twelve-cylinder rakish sport car, and spent much of their free time polishing it and pleasure driving through the San Francisco hill streets, and exploring the back roads in Marin County across the bay.

John by now had become assertive enough against his father's paternal dominance, to talk Dan into going to San Francisco, too, to see if they could not do better there.

When John joined his brothers in San Francisco, it was a joyous occasion. The three of them were young and carefree. San Francisco, at that time, was a small metropolis that was truly a city of romance, with its cable cars to Nob Hill, China Town, the Golden Gate Park, Fisherman's Wharf, and the azure bay laced with ferries and cargo ships plying to and from their berths. The two great cable bridges to span the bay were yet in their planning stages.

John rented a room near North Beach in an old but well-kept hotel for fifty cents a night. Dan soon found a job in South San Francisco, working for a woman with some kind of racetrack concession, and moved out, leaving John by himself for the first time in his life. He was eighteen years old with less than a grammar school education and no marketable skills. He unpacked his belongings, which consisted of a few clothes and his one most precious valuable: a worn dog-eared Webster's dictionary, which he had acquired while at Sardine Creek to aid in his reading while there. He referred to the dictionary often and even listed words to learn, for he was acutely aware and ashamed of his academic ignorance from his long years of isolation.

The first event to enter his life in San Francisco was an enteric germ, an annoying and prolonged attack of diarrhea that began to worry him. The illness was physically weakening and prevented him from looking for a job. After a few days, he decided something had to be done about the diarrhea.

Frantically he looked through the Yellow Pages of the phone book for the name of a doctor near to where he lived, and he found that there was a doctor's clinic only a couple of city blocks away. John found the place and entered into a generous-sized waiting room in which he was surprised to notice all the patients were women. He gave his name to the receptionist and was told to wait to be called into the doctor's office. He gradually became aware that the ladies were all looking at him peculiarly and he began feeling rather uncomfortable, especially since his gut was writhing at the same time. Eventually he was called to the doctor's examining room and was again surprised that the doctor, too, was a neatly dressed, middle-aged woman in a prim business suit. The doctor was flanked by a pretty young nurse in an impeccable uniform and nurse's cap.

The doctor asked, "What can I do for you, young man?"

John explained with some embarrassment that he had a prolonged case of dysentery that wouldn't stop. Doctor and nurse exchanged bemused glances.

"Why did you come here?" the doctor asked.

John explained that he had looked in the phone book for the nearest doctor to where he lived.

The doctor nodded knowingly and said, "Do you know what kind of a doctor I am?" John admitted that he did not.

"I am a doctor of gynecology and obstetrics," she said.

John, with his limited sexual knowledge, had no idea what that was, so the only appropriate response he could think of was to say, "Oh."

But John made a mental note that as soon as he got back to his room he would look up this strange title in his dog-eared dictionary.

By now both doctor and nurse were looking at each other with bemused expressions.

"Sure, I can help you," the doctor sympathetically assured him, and she wrote out a list of foods he was to eat and the name of a medicine to get at a pharmacy. When John left the clinic, he noticed that as he walked through the waiting room, the eyes of every young woman followed him as if he was the participant in a tennis match and they were all following the action. Then for the first time he also noticed the bulging abdomens of some of the ladies, and it finally came to his consciousness that in his innocent ignorance he had made some kind of faux pas. Back in the privacy of his room, he got out his dictionary and looked up the word "gynecology." He muttered to himself, "So that was what that was all about!" His sex education was accruing in sudden jerks.

After exhausting all of his money down to a remaining fifteen cents and then being robbed of that by a pickpocket, John found a job parking cars in a parking lot for fifty cents a day, and additional money could be earned wax-polishing cars for twenty cents each. He found that he could work his way through about five cars each day for a total salary of a whole dollar and a half. John felt fortunate to have such a good job. It nicely paid all of his living expenses.

In San Francisco in 1935, a person could see a good movie for ten cents, and John found that for thirty-five cents he could get a whopping big T-bone steak in a somewhat greasy Greek restaurant on Mission Street, or a large satisfying bowl of curry and chicken for fifteen cents at an East Indian restaurant on Howard Street, or all the chow mein you could eat for a dime at a Chinese restaurant on Stockton Street, and for a nickel you could travel on a street car anywhere in the city.

The auto parking lot where John worked was at the end of Market Street within sight of the famous San Francisco Ferry Building, which was still a beehive of activity, with colorful ferries criss-crossing the bay, bound for Oakland or Sausalito. The parking lot was leased by a warm-hearted old Swedish couple who were childless and treated John as if he were their own son.

Dan worked at his new job for a while when he began drinking heavily again and was promptly fired. He returned and stayed with John while looking for another job. At an employment agency, he applied for a job as the caretaker of an estate in Benbow, California, in the Redwood forest region of Humbolt County. The wealthy owner of the estate was an elderly unmarried lady, Miss Stewart, who was co-owner with her brother of the San Francisco Stewart Hotel—a luxury hotel that largely served foreign travelers and affluent tourists.

Miss Margaret Stewart was very proud of her Scottish ancestry, and very attendant to the traditions and lore of the Scottish clans. With her penchant for Celtic culture, it was natural for her to be attracted to the Scottish name "Macdonald." Dan did not disillusion Miss Stewart by telling her it was an adopted name that came from his stepfather, William Macdonald, and that he may or may not have had Scottish ancestors, for he was unsure of his ancestry. He needed a job too much to burden her with any extra information. He qualified himself as having years of experience in the nursery and floral business, and that was all true. Miss Stewart hired him with great enthusiasm, obviously charmed to have a Scottish gardener.

Dan and John once more packed all of their worldly belongings, consisting mostly of a few clothes, into the old Nash touring car and headed north out of San Francisco, crossing the bay on a car ferry and headed for the redwoods of northern California. The winter weather was briskly cold, and that day there were scudding clouds gathering for a storm. All went well till they reached the little town of Willits, about fifty miles short of their destination at Benbow. Suddenly something clanked in the transmission and the car came to a stop. Dan called on the services of a local garage mechanic, who diagnosed the problem as a broken gear. A new replacement part, Dan was told, was probably not available for such an old vehicle.

Neither of them had the money to pay the cost of the

repairs anyway, so they just walked away from the 1926 Nash touring car that had brought the family out from Michigan, leaving its rusty decrepit body abandoned beside the redwood highway. The two of them took their few clothes and belongings and hitchhiked the remainder of the trip to Benbow.

Winter in the redwoods in 1935 did not draw many travelers, so the hitchhiking consisted mostly of hiking and very little hitching. The raw cold weather added to their discomfort. By the time they reached Benbow, they were both suffering from a condition close to hypothermia, but what followed, socially speaking, was even colder. They were met at the Stewart estate, by the former caretaker, Mr. Gray, who had been carrying on an imbroglio with Miss Stewart, and she had fired him.

Mr. Gray, a handsome and impeccably dressed man with the decorum of a country gentleman and a somewhat self-aggrandized demeanor, vented his anger with Miss Stewart, against Dan. As cold and miserable as he and John were, Mr. Gray would not let them on the premises. After some negotiations he relented enough to let them sleep in the basement of the main house. Mr. Gray's caretaker quarters was in a bachelor apartment over the garage, which he would not give up. They spent that night, which was cold and threatening rain, on a damp cement basement floor without access to either food or warmth.

During the night, John, peering through a tiny basement window, imagined he saw a ghost, but it turned out to be Mr. Gray's suit of long underwear hanging on an outdoors clothesline, with the arms and legs twirling in the wan night light, in a slow dance from the wind. From time to time, coyotes across the river were exchanging their yelping communications as the eerie moon sought to find holes between the fast moving clouds. Whenever the coyotes barked, Mr. Gray's huge German shepherd added a low melancholy and mournful howl. The Gothic aura was unsettling to John.

Dan and John, the next morning, were greatly relieved to observe that Mr. Gray was packing up to move out. He asked Dan to care for his dog, named "Hero." It was a name that seemed to personify the master as somewhat gushy and excessive. Surely the dog would have been ashamed of his name had he been aware of its meaning. The dog was in fact a very intelligent playful monster, more like a cheery buffoon than a hero.

In the light of the day, with a winter sun beaming down on them, they explored the premises and found that they were in a jewel of a setting. The estate was on three acres of landscaped gardens bordering the Eel River. There were two separate houses, the main house and a smaller guest house. Dan and John had their own comfortable bachelor apartment to live in over the large garage.

The English Tudor houses were artfully faced in cut stone, and following the graceful curves of the river was a long stone wall overgrown with English ivy. One could sit atop the wall and observe a mile or more span up and down the peaceful Eel. The other side of the river was arched over with massive redwood trees above, garlands of vine maple and huckleberry bushes below, and underfoot was an age-old carpet of redwood mulch and sphagnum moss where you tread in hushed silence in respect for the majesty of the forest.

In the basement of the house was a steam boiler for heating and a generous sized workshop. Upstairs on the main floor, covered with protective sheets, were tasteful old world Queen Anne and Chippendale furniture. There were silken draped windows, and embossed papered walls hung with paintings, original oils and water colors. There was a modern kitchen and a large dining room, plus a warm picture-windowed breakfast room overlooking the gardens. There was a music room large enough to accommodate a small chamber orchestra, and there was an enormous Steinway grand electric player piano. Upstairs were generous-sized bedrooms and baths, and a warm sun deck facing the river. John had never seen such luxury in his entire life before. Walking through the vacant house and across the plushy deep carpets instilled in him a somber mood as in the silence of a church. The quietness of the place with its impressive setting produced an ambiguous feeling of a dream world that could vanish upon awakening.

John could not help but compare this Elysian estate house designed by the distinguished California architect Julia Morgan* to the cabin on Sardine Creek where only a short time before he lived and starved for years in a rough-hewn shack with tin can lids nailed over knotholes in the floor. It was hard to adjust to this Cinderella fantasy. It was a shock to his senses. To lower the level of nervous feeling, he made friends with the dog "Hero," whose unassuming character made anyone who played with him a lifelong friend, if they just entered into his frisky happy game of chasing sticks thrown into the river.

The guest house was a warm, cozy two-bedroom tastefully furnished house with complete kitchen and a nice breakfast room, a large living room with fireplace, and a long veranda porch overlooking the river. The land on which the houses were located was enclosed in a high chain link fence for security and was approached by a winding gravel drive that connected to a little used secondary road leading to the redwood highway.

*Morgan designed and directed the construction of Hearst's Castle in San Simeon, California.

When Dan had taken the job in San Francisco, he was instructed by Miss Stewart, a somewhat confused dowager of about eighty years, to check the whole household inventory immediately from a list he was provided. She did not trust Mr. Gray. Accordingly within a day of settling in, they began the inventory job. Before an hour was up, they found in alarm that a lot of pieces of furniture, vases, pictures, and bric-a-brac were all missing. Dan suggested that perhaps Mr. Gray had been selling the furniture.

Dan caught a ride into Garberville, the nearest town, to telephone Miss Stewart. There was no telephone in the house at Benbow. Dan reported that there were all sorts of things missing from the inventory. Miss Stewart answered the phone. She was a little confused by what he was saying. She referred him to talk to her hotel purchasing agent who was more familiar with the inventory. It turned out that the purchasing agent, a sharp and efficient German, knew all about the missing items. Some had been taken out of the house and put into the winter house in Carmel, and some were in the penthouse in San Francisco. Miss Stewart, in her advanced age, didn't really know what she owned and was too muddled to care anyway.

Much relieved, Dan returned to Benbow and he and John settled in to enjoy their first really fortunate circumstances since leaving Michigan in 1929. There was not much maintenance work for them to do during the winter months. They occupied themselves keeping house and exploring the area.

The Benbow Hotel, about a half mile upstream on the river from them, was a magnificent English half-timber and cut stone luxury establishment built in 1926. All the stone masonry was overseen by an excellent stone mason who had also done the masonry for the Stewart estate, and whose past apprenticeship had never been made very clear to the Benbow family.

When the job was finished, it was said that the stone mason kited his last pay check by adding a zero or two. In the subsequent investigation, it was found that his fine masonry skills were learned in a Florida prison camp doing stone-cutting.

Downstream from the hotel about three miles was a low profile hydroelectric power producing dam. The dam was built in such a way that during the summer tourist season, when the river flow was at its minimum, a ten-foot-high bulkhead dam could be erected atop the basic concrete dam to raise the water level higher to form a nice seasonal lake for boating and swimming. Across the top of the dam was a long swaying cable foot bridge by which the river could be crossed to get to the electric generator room and the salmon fish ladders. John was intrigued by the area. There had been a successful blending of modern technology and rustic beauty that was not out of harmony with each other.

In the decade of the depression years, almost no tourists visited the redwoods during the winter months. Local residents shut their doors to the deluge of winter rains and occupied themselves by making redwood knickknacks to sell during the following tourist seasons. The Benbow Hotel was locked up, and so few people were about that it was like a season of hibernation. The only activity was a few operating lumber mills that little by little were eating away at destroying one of the most fantastic gardens of nature that the world had ever produced.

Between rain storms, John would often cross the cable bridge at the Benbow Dam and hike into the two- or three-thousand-year-old forest bordering the Eel River. The ancient accumulated forest mulch formed a rich soil out of which giant woodwardia ferns reached to the shoulders of a hiker, amid rambling vine maple and huckleberry bushes. Set apart at stately intervals, the redwood trees reached to the sun and air hundreds of feet above. John was awed by the auspicious size of the trees, and his mind complied to the mood of the forest by welling up thoughts of reverence akin to being in church.

But the beauty of the forest evoked loneliness, too, a feeling of subdued humility in the presence of such grandeur. After his long trial of privation and hunger through the years of the Great Depression, this place appeared to him as if he had reached a calm safe harbor. In this tree cathedral setting, he could not help but contemplate the creative urge of nature that brought all of this magnificence into being—such beauty, such control, such omnipotence has to come out of a creative force that regulates the universe from the micro atoms to the macro stars. He began to think about his relationship with this Supreme Regulatory Being. He began to wonder why he was here, what were the purposes of these complex forces that had shaped both him and the fantasia world he was observing. He began to see that mankind is only a tiny thread in the warp and weft of the tapestry of the universe, and he a fiber of the thread.

It occurred to John that the special attributes of mankind, human consciousness and intelligence, is a symbiotic resource to be used to support and augment the Creator's cosmic art. In coming to these conclusions, he became peacefully reconciled with his personal experiences of both joy and hardship in his past life. He was learning to regard the lifetime spectrum of physical and emotional ventures as like a personal biblical text. He concluded that all people's lives are their personal biblical text from which to grow a meaningful existence. The magnificent ecology of the redwood forest had become his learning lab, and the world of nature had become his temple of worship. Well it would be that that temple should inspire the human race in a seamless uncompetitive universal religion of ecological veneration of the spirit that quickened the universe. His mentor had become the seventeenth century Jewish philosopher, Spinoza, who asserted nature and the Divine mind are one and the same.

16

As the winter of 1935 progressed, the rainforest produced its normal regimen of storm after storm swelling the Eel River to overflow into all of its flood plains. People without strong inner resources may suffer melancholy and loneliness during the incessant and somber rains, but John was happy and content. It was a period of spiritual awakening for him.

There were always interesting observations to be made of the ravages of the flooding river. One morning John observed an entire chicken house complete with all the chickens riding on the roof, floating down the Eel. From time to time, the structure would crash into a floating log jam, whereupon the distraught chickens would make awkward flights up from the roof of their house in a flutter of feathers, and then settle down again to ride their little island to the sea, seemingly a likely parable of human destiny, a flutter of activity in the vast current of creation.

The drenching winter rains of the redwood forest climate have produced the sustaining phloem that has nourished their gigantic splendor for thousands of years, but for those persons who do not understand their ecology, and who do not surrender to it passively, it produces a gloomy torpor. Dan became restless and bored by the days and months of incessant deluges. He and John began a tournament of playing checkers while the rains poured down.

Each evening they would play a little later into the

night, and each morning rise a bit later in the morning. Before many days had gone by they found that the drifting schedule had reversed their normal regimen; they were playing checkers all night and sleeping all day.

With very little work to occupy his time, John again took up studying words in his dog-eared dictionary. He felt a deep uneasy awareness of his lack of education that had abruptly been cut off at age twelve. The Book of the Month Club had been established about this time, and he became a member with the initial free volume of H. G. Wells, *Science of Life*. He bought an Underwood portable typewriter and taught himself to type. He started a diary.

When the rains finally dried up and spring arrived, the Benbows put the ten-foot bulkhead in the Eel River dam, raising the river into an attractive lake for fishing and canoeing, but also creating a barrier for the migrating eels coming upstream from the ocean, the eels for which the river was named.

Miss Stewart came up from San Francisco with an entire entourage of people, including a Filipino cook, a female companion, a secretary, and three of her brother's children, with their English nanny. Suddenly, the place was a bustle of activity.

Miss Stewart called Dan in to consult with him about the gardens and upkeep of the property. She was a peppery but kindly old lady, and a little confused, forgetting each day what she had told him the day before. The summer was warm and pleasant, and John felt fortunate at having adequate food, clothing, and shelter, in contrast to the terrible previous years of the Great Depression that had seemed like they would be endless.

During the summer, John became quite well acquainted with Miss Stewart's female secretary, a somewhat lonely middle-aged single woman. She sensed John's anxiety about his lack of education. She urged him to write letters to her through the following winter, whereupon she would correct the spelling, punctuation, and language, and return the letters to him to improve his English. It was probably the equivalent of a good high-school English course for which he was ever after grateful of her kindness.

In the autumn of 1936, the young Stewarts took their family back to San Francisco, and the elderly Miss Stewart returned to her penthouse atop the Stewart Hotel. John and his father were alone again for the oncoming winter. They began the season's activity by building a wharf on the river front and a rowboat to tie up to the wharf. During the construction, Dan fell into the river one day while cutting down an overhanging tree. He had never learned to swim, and it was in water about ten feet deep.

In spite of the deep water, he managed to paddle ashore and even save the saw. It was a remarkable feat, made even more remarkable by a subsequent event of the same nature the following year.

During the winter John found another activity. He loved classical music, and he found that the Stewarts' music room contained multitudes of piano rolls of the world's finest artists, and they could be played on the Grand Steinway electric player piano. From these recitals he became desirous of learning to play. He bought a home instruction course to teach himself, but he quickly found it is one thing to love music and quite another thing to learn to play music. He had no talent for this whole new language of notes and quickly gave up the ambition.

The forlorn days of winter rain began again, gloomy days for local people sheltered in their houses, but glistening days for the redwood trees, their serrated heavy bark absorbing life-giving rain, turning the tree trunks dark umber, and streaming the water down into the deep mulch of the forest floor. Day by day the Eel River crept higher on its embankments. That winter the Benbows kept waiting for a break in the weather to remove the bulkheads from the dam, but no break ever came. Then the heavens split asunder and a pouring deluge dramatically struck the already flooded river. Great amounts of driftwood began backing up behind the bulkhead till a critical mass occurred and the whole top of the dam gave away, twisting twelve-inch steel I-beams over like hairpins.

The whole bulkhead portion of the dam was swept away. The power of the river was awesome. The little dory boat that Dan and John had built was torn from its mooring and lost, but the wharf they had built held in place.

The sodden rains continued to pour down that winter with monotonous regularity. Animals may crawl back into their lairs during storms and live comfortably on their fat, but the human spirit turns in upon itself, generating an irritable burden of wet clothing, stuck in the mud cars, and dreary chores. Dan was not spiritually girded to patiently outwait the weather. He began going into town and buying quantities of beer and keeping himself in a constant alcoholic ennui.

It was now just before the summer season and the return of the Stewarts. The gardens were neglected and in disarray, the sun porch of the main house had been leaking and caused damage, the house itself was damp and musty. When Miss Stewart arrived on the scene, she called Dan in and fired him. But she called him in again the following day and told him in glowing terms what she expected him to do during the next year. Perhaps she was kindly forgiving, or maybe because of her advanced age, she just forgot that she had fired him the day before. On the whole it was another pleasant summer that John enjoyed.

John began finding other people in the Benbow area who had summer homes that needed attending to and was picking up odds and ends jobs that kept him busy and in spending money.

It was now the winter of 1937. Hitler's storm trooper activities in Germany were ominous. President Roosevelt was beginning to try to lead the nation away from isolation in foreign affairs. A battle of wills erupted in the auto industry between the United Auto Workers and Henry Ford. Dan predicted there would be a terrible war before long. The economic depression was still having its effect, now in its seventh year. But there was a renewed economic movement abroad by all the nations of Europe rearming themselves against the threat of war.

When the winter rains came again, Dan fell into a depressed mood and began keeping himself constantly intoxicated during the dreary months. When his last great entrepreneurship adventure had failed, the gold mine on Sardine Creek, it had taken his spirit with it and he had not been able to find a new goal since then. His wife was dead and his children scattered and no longer looking to him for nurture. Life had beaten him down. He had been a man who depended on the energy generated by enterprising dreams and optimism, and optimism had died for everyone during the Great Depression.

There was a family who owned a large department store in San Francisco that had a beautiful Spanish Villa house near Benbow. They only occupied it during the summer months, and John had been hired to look after it during the winter. Vandalism was a problem among the isolated summer homes. John drove over to the Hale house one gray day and spent an hour or two gardening.

Dan was in a depressed mood and had been drinking heavily for several days on an extended alcoholic binge. When John returned, his father was nowhere about. John assumed he had just gone into Garberville for another supply of beer. After several hours went by, John became disturbed by the long absence. He began searching the place and hiked down to the wharf. There he was surprised to find their new dory boat untied and freely floating against the dock with the wind holding it in place.

When evening came and Dan still did not show up, John called the sheriff's department in some alarm. They advised him to wait till morning and suggested he might be sleeping out somewhere. But John was convinced that something was wrong. He waited all night and called the sheriff again in the morning. An officer came out to search the premises, but Dan could not be found anywhere. John mentioned about the boat being untied. They walked down to the dock together. The early morning lake water was as clear as glass.

Peering down through the deep water beside the wharf, John saw his father's body on the lake bottom. It was like the suddenness of an electric shock. To John, his father was as permanent in his mind as the land. That he could have drowned at the wharf-side was incredible. His father had seemed like an entity larger than life, an immortal man. John was stunned. His first reaction was anger and he blamed his father for what had happened. Then immediately he felt lonely. Suddenly he realized he had no close support person any longer.

His father, who had been the most important person in his life for twenty years, suddenly within a day was gone.

The fragility of life is most impressive by its passage.

A coroner's investigation revealed a very high blood alcohol content, and there were no marks on his body from any kind of injury. They surmised that he had untied the boat and fell into the water while trying to get into it. Perhaps because of mental depression, he did not try to save himself. It may have been partly accident and partly suicidal resignation that took his life at age fifty-nine. A life cycle had been completed in which Dan's death was seemingly almost identical to his father's death by drowning in a lake in Canada in 1879.

John notified his sister Helen in Klamath Falls, Oregon, his brother Dave in San Francisco, and Ron—newly married—in Gaviota, California. The children all gathered at the Stewart place to plan and attend the last rites of their father. Together they made a decision to make a floral blanket to cover his casket, in memory of the many times they had all worked together with their father doing the same kind of work, at Macdonald's Farm many years before. As sad as the circumstances were, there was yet an aura of happiness and closure for the children similar to that of a funeral wake. John felt that his father would have approved of the mood. The children had not all come together like this for years past, and that togetherness in itself buoyed their spirits.

The funeral was conducted by the Masonic Lodge at a little cemetery on a flood plain on the Eel River near Miranda, California, close to the Avenue of the Giants parkway. Years later the flooding Eel River overran the cemetery and removed all traces of the burial site.

After the funeral the family members returned to their various homes and John remained at Benbow, at the kind forbearance of the Stewarts. He stayed through the following summer and then made a decision to leave the redwood forests, even though here he had experienced the greatest contentment of his life up to that time. Surely nowhere on earth is there a more beautiful place to live one's youth than among the giant forests of Humbolt County. But he had reached a passage and it was time to move on. It was the season of life for the process of maturity to begin. John made a decision to return to San Francisco.

17

With great excitement John bought his first car to drive to San Francisco and also had his first experience with a used-car dealer. The car he chose was a Dodge pickup truck that had been in an accident and so was priced to sell well below the market value for that model, an excellent buy he was assured by the salesman. It was a sweltering hot day, so the windows were down in the truck cab to keep it cool. John concentrated on the engine, revving it up to see how it sounded, and looked for oil leaks. The salesman assured him there would be thousands of miles of good transportation in this vehicle with no problems. It was so hot he left the windows down till he got home. Only then did he discover that the car had no windows. They had been broken out in the accident and not replaced—so that was really why the windows were down. A complaint to the salesman brought the response that he had never said it had window glass in it. That was John's problem.

John's trip to San Francisco took him across the Golden Gate Bridge, the first time he had seen this gigantic but graceful structure strung across the entrance to one of the world's greatest harbors. The bridge had only been opened to traffic the year before. He had been told to rent a room in the old tenement district on upper Mission Street. The buildings in the area were almost all identical, typical San Francisco apartment houses built in the early twenties with projecting sun-seeking dormer windows and worn walk-up concrete stairs. Upper apartments had little outdoor balconies adorned with scraggly geraniums struggling to survive.

When John found the apartment house, which had been recommended by his brother Dave, he ran up the flight of outdoor concrete steps and tried the door. The ancient doorknob simply turned around and around without unlatching the door. He pushed the call bell button, also without success. John tried the doorknob several times, again with no success at opening the door. He was about to leave when some children, playing in the street, began laughing at his frustration. A little girl came to his rescue and instructed him to pull the doorknob toward him hard while turning it. Sure enough, the door unlatched for him to enter.

In the hall he met Maria, the proprietor. John, with annoyance, asked why she didn't get the door fixed. Her answer was that all her renters knew how to open the door and she didn't want it fixed. It was her way of keeping drunks off the street from entering the apartment at night. Maria, a disheveled middle-aged woman with obvious henna-dyed hair and a "You-all" Southern accent, gave him a tour. John was struck by the musty odor and sour smell of stale tobacco smoke saturated in the carpets and walls. This first floor of the building had a long straight hall passing clear through to the rear of the building, and off of the hall were separate little single rooms like a hotel.

Maria leased this floor of the apartment house only. In the basement was a Chinese laundry, and upstairs on the second floor were whole family apartments, with a different tenant who then subrented to families. Plumbing and wiring were of vintage design and of questionable reliability. John's room was squalid but functional, and what could he expect for twenty dollars a month?

After settling in, John soon became accustomed to the neighborhood lifestyle: Almost daily he could hear a next-door neighbor woman shrieking and crying as she was being beaten by her husband, while on the floor above, an accordion student was ripping out the melody of "You are my sunshine—my only sunshine."

John's next priority was to set about finding a job. Taking a cue from his brother Dave, he applied successfully for an apprenticeship job at a local scale company on Howard Street. They only had about a dozen employees, so everyone knew each other with a friendly intimacy that John enjoyed. It was almost like a family. He soon discovered that repairing and adjusting scales got him into almost every industrial plant and food store in the city, for rarely is there a business that does not weigh some product that requires accurate scales. His favorite was Ghirardelli's Chocolate Factory down on the waterfront. Ghirardelli's was one of San Francisco's oldest and renowned business establishments. They hired many women workers and that was an added attraction to repairing their scales. Almost always, after doing his work, the women would fill a paper sack for him with a generous supply of chunks of delicious baker's chocolate.

Maria, John's landlady, also had a little café across the street from her rooming house, where she urged her tenants to partake of Southern fried chicken and Oklahoma cuisine. John found the food and the premises all a bit greasy, but tolerable for the price.

One evening John was having his supper at Maria's Café when across the counter from him he could not help but notice a very pretty young woman of about his own age. There was a firmness and yet a humorous expression in the set of her mouth and the arch of her eyes. A puff of brown curls framed her forehead. She wore a conservative business suit, and her only feminine ornamentation was a pair of teardrop gold earrings. Because of her attractiveness, John kept looking over at her again and again. He soon observed that she was a tense person from the way she kept moving her hands, shoving bits of food about on her plate with her fork. She dug into a small purse and pulled out a package of cigarettes, expertly popped one out, rapped it on the back of her hand, placed the tip of it in her mouth, touched a lighter flame to the tobacco, and drew in a deep inhalation of smoke. She was obviously amused at a story that another patron was telling her, and she suddenly broke into a wide laugh that was like the sun coming out. John was entranced as he watched her inhale smoke and then playfully tap her cheek with her forefinger, producing a myriad of little smoke rings.

After she left John asked Maria who the pretty girl was.

"That is Margie," Maria said. "She has rented a room from me."

Margie began eating meals daily at the café, and each day as he lunched, John marveled at the square cut of her jaw, the flawless skin, the arch of the brow, the warm brown eyes, the poise and self-confidence of her demeanor, the lovely figure, the flair of her clothing.

John kept conjecturing as to how he could go about getting to know this beautiful girl. His years of isolation and lonely existence had left him almost bereft of social skills. Desperately he concocted a plan of just setting down beside her, making a friendly remark, and seeing what would happen. It took uncommon courage to be so bold. He even dressed for the occasion and wore a necktie, an article of enhancement that he would never wear ordinarily.

When she came into the café he timed himself to quickly sit down beside her before the stool was occupied by anyone else. But then he couldn't think of anything to say to her. They ordered their food and both ate in silence. She lit up a cigarette, blew out a cloud of smoke, looked at him with interest, and then pointed out to John, "Your tie is in your mashed potatoes."

John retrieved his tie with humiliation and stammered that he hadn't noticed. Casting about for some way to start a conversation, he thought perhaps the weather might give him an opening. He said to her, "It's foggy out—but that's San Francisco."

Margie looked at him quizzically and a little amused.

"You're right," she said, "It is foggy out." She mashed her cigarette into the leftover food on her plate and turned to converse with a friend on the other side of her. John felt an acute sense of failure.

The next time he saw Margie in the café, she was dressed in a form-fitting pants suit that displayed every feminine curve. Her one ornamentation was an orange scarf that set off her flawless skin. She appeared anxious and nervous, smoking one cigarette after another.

Suddenly there was an earsplitting roar of a motorcycle coming to a fast stop across from the café. John observed the driver to be a solid muscular young man with a long scraggly mop of dark hair and a woolly beard. He was wearing a black leather jacket and faded jeans with a brass-studded belt about two inches wide and high-heeled cowboy boots. From clear across the street, the rider made a beckoning wave toward the café. Margie mashed out her cigarette, ran out the door, and over to the motorcyclist. Without hesitation she swung her leg over the saddle behind the driver, and put her arms about his waist. The driver throttled up the engine and with an earth-shattering roar, they flew up Mission Street with shrieking tire rubber. John wondered if he would ever see Margie again. But in the coming weeks, the motorcycle episode became an ongoing routine affair. John mused to himself, how could he ever compete for Margie's attention against this hairy masculine motorcycle gladiator? He gave up in resignation.

Several months went by and the motorcycle guy came again and again to pick up Margie. He never got off of his bike and came into the café to greet her. He just beckoned to her to come to him from clear across the street.

Margie always responded with the same good cheer, going to him like a moth travels to a candle. John in his uncertainty and inexperience with girls, could not help but wonder if this boorish behavior was the new acceptable way of wooing, but evidently Margie loved it, for she never failed to ride off on the motorized steed, gripping her boyfriend's brass-studded belt.

One day as John was sitting in Maria's Café, dawdling over a cup of coffee, a yellow cab drew up to the curb in front of the apartment house. The door of the cab was hurriedly thrown open and Margie quickly got out and tossed the driver some money. Without waiting for her change, she ran up the steps to the apartment door. John could see immediately that something was wrong with her. She turned the door knob to enter and of course it just turned around and around without unlatching the door. She screamed out an unearthly shriek and yelled, "Shit!" Then John noticed there was blood flowing down her legs. He ran across the street, grabbed the door knob, pulled and turned at the same time, and the door opened. Margie ran in and raced down the hall, screaming, "Maria!"

Maria came out of a side door, took one look, grabbed Margie's arm, and led her to her room, slamming the bedroom door behind her. There was a few minutes of silence and then Maria rushed out into the hall and down to the public phone. She called General Hospital for an ambulance and urged them to hurry.

Noticing John for the first time, Maria blurted out, "The stupid girl! She did this to herself."

Some time passed before they carried Margie out on a stretcher with a blanket over her, to the waiting ambulance. John was shocked at the turn of events.

Two days later, he asked Maria if she thought it would be all right for him to visit Margie at General Hospital.

"That would be nice," Maria assured him. "You might bring her a few flowers and something to read. She'd probably like that."

John carefully selected a little bouquet of violets at a florist shop. He wondered what kind of reading she might enjoy and selected a copy of *The Ladies Home Journal*.

18

John found Margie propped up in bed, but looking somewhat pale. Her eyes, normally so bright and warm, were dull and spiritless, but she smiled when he entered the room. She took the violets, smelled their fragrance, and said, "God, I wish I had a cigarette. They won't let me smoke." She looked over the magazine, laid it aside, and glancing up at him, commented, "I guess I'm not the *Ladies Home Journal* type, but thank you. It was thoughtful."

Casting about for something to say, John asked, "Has the motorcycle guy been in to see you?"

"No," she said flatly, "the motorcycle guy has not come in to see me. Probably the motorcycle guy will never come in to see me," she said bitterly.

"When can you go home?" John inquired.

"Saturday," she answered.

"Can I take you home?" John inquired.

She looked interested and answered, "Yes, that would be helpful."

When Saturday came, John, with great anticipation, brought her out to his pickup truck and bundled her into the car with her few belongings.

Before starting out, he asked with some anxiety, "Would you like to go to a movie?" It seemed to him like a somewhat brazen suggestion, so he was expecting a "no thanks."

To his surprise she answered, "Sure, why not?"

He drove down to "The President's Theater," a new modern establishment at that time, which later burned up from a fire in the projection room. Tickets were twenty cents each and for that nominal amount, they saw two full-length feature films, a Pathé news film, and a Disney comedy, about five hours of entertainment, with dishes given away in between features to those with a lucky number on their ticket stubs.

When they left the theater, John asked Margie if she was hungry.

"Famished," she said.

He took her to Clifton's Cafeteria on Market Street, and there he ordered his favorite specialty: Clifton's hash and eggs. Margie had the same meal and they relaxed in a genial mood. John noticed that there was no playing with her food as she did before her miscarriage, or abortion, or whatever. She ate with obvious relish, and they topped off the meal with another Clifton's specialty: tapioca pudding.

John asked, "Were you born in San Francisco?"

"Oh no," she answered. "I came here from Chicago." She went on to tell him her story: She had no brothers or sisters. Her father was a shoe salesmen in Chicago, and a heavy drinker.

"Mother and Father quarreled endlessly," she said. When she was eight, her mother just ran off one day and disappeared. Because he was Catholic, her father refused to get a divorce. Instead he put Margie in a Catholic boarding school and lived a lonely life by himself.

When her father left her at the boarding school, he paid her tuition and gave the Sister Superior a hundred dollars that was to be used for any special things that his daughter might need.

It was a gloomy and very unhappy time in Margie's

life. Every day, every week, every month she waited for her father to return to take her away, but it never happened. He did visit her from time to time, usually on holidays, but even these visits became ever more infrequent and on several occasions, he was obviously drunk and had a sleazy woman with him.

Margie grew to hate the nuns. Their assumption seemed to be that all the girls were naturally evil and had to be trained to be moral through catechism, prayer, and lectures.

They had a clever tiny dwarfed girl who was spirited, clownish, and full of the devil, as Margie put it. The girls loved to put her up to various mischief. So the nuns called her "the devil girl" and the schoolgirls promptly named her "DG." DG sought the attention and approval of her classmates by acting as their prankster.

The girls stole an office key and they talked DG into sneaking into the school office at night to steal packages of cigarettes out of the nun's supply. The girls would take the cigarettes into the rest room and light up, with DG standing guard outside to whistle a hymn if a nun came to investigate. When they heard the whistled signal, everyone threw their cigarettes into a toilet and flushed it. The sisters entering would see great clouds of smoke but no smokers—all the girls looking very innocent. But one time Sister Superior did a search of all their blouses and found a package of cigarettes hidden in Margie's blouse. It happened that the girls were scheduled to have a beach party at Lake Michigan. As punishment, Sister Superior grounded Margie, and she was the only one left alone at the school.

Angry and disappointed, she searched DG's belongings and found the key to the office, entered and rifled through Sister Superior's desk for cigarettes. To Margie's surprise, she ran across an envelope with her name on it in her father's handwriting. The envelope had a hundred dollars in it, the money her father had left her years before for whatever special and personal needs she might have. She never had been given a penny of her own money. Margie made a decision right then to take her own money and run away. She was sixteen years old at the time. She removed her school uniform, dressed in street clothes, and left the school. She found the Greyhound bus station and bought a one-way ticket to San Francisco, as far as she could get from Chicago.

John listened to the story with rapt attention, and felt exaltation at her courage to run away—an act he could never have brought himself to do even as abused as he was in his childhood.

He took Margie back to their Mission Street run-down Victorian apartment house and left her at her door. He had a strong urge to give her a good-night kiss, but was just too timid to try it—but in the back of his mind, an idea formed: "Tomorrow is Sunday," he said. "Why don't we pack a lunch and drive up Twin Peaks for a picnic?"

Margie squeezed his hand. "You're nice, but I go to church Sunday morning, and in the afternoon I need to do my laundry."

In surprise, John asked, "You attend church?"

Seeing the disappointment in his face, Margie added, "But we can go in the afternoon after I finish my chores."

"Fine," said John. "I'll pack a lunch and pick you up at five."

Margie looked amused. "Let me pack the lunch," she said.

Sunday afternoon, John bundled Margie into the pickup truck and they drove up the Twin Peaks road above the scattered houses to the unpaved parking lot near the crest overlooking the whole city. It happened that it was during one of those rare weather conditions called a "Santa Ana" in which a high pressure mass of air over central California produces hot offshore winds that sweep the coastal fog out to sea and leave the city air crystal clear. They sat together enjoying the scene and the lunch.

John said, "I was surprised that you go to church. Do you believe in all that Catholic stuff?"

Margie looked a little apprehensive. "What do you mean? I believe in God."

"But you said you hated catechism and all that stuff."

"I hated the nuns," she said. "I love the church. Don't you believe in God?"

"Well, yes," John admitted, "but I don't think it is like your God. I believe that God is in nature," and he gestured toward the panoramic view before them. "I believe like the great philosopher Spinoza."

"Who is Spinoza?" Margie asked.

"He was a Jewish theologian who lived in the seventeenth century. He said that nature and the Divine mind were the same."

"I don't think that can be so," Margie objected. "God has to be greater than nature. He has to be outside of nature if He created nature."

"But how do you know He created nature?" John asked. "Why can't nature and the mind of God be exactly the same thing?"

"Because," Margie answered, "my church says that God is a supreme being or spirit, and that all of nature is created by that spirit. All of this," and she gestured out toward the great bay, "did not make itself by spontaneous generation."

"But if that is so," John sid, "we must not have any free will, and we just live a preprogramed destiny that God created in a preprogramed universe. And besides, what about all those poor miserable children who are born deformed, or blind, or deaf? Does God plan that, too?"

Margie looked disturbed. "Of course not," she said. "The world is a place where both good and bad reside at the same time, and we are here to practice the good."

John said, "How do you know always what is good and what is bad? Sometimes what is good for me is bad for others."

"For that purpose we have the Scripture and our Catechism," Margie answered.

"All that stuff doesn't impress me," John said.

"What stuff?" Margie demanded.

"Things like those little soda crackers the priest puts in your mouth, and that wine business."

"It's symbolic of Christ's blood and body," said Margie defensively. "It's called holy communion. That is what all Catholics have in common and it gives us a feeling of togetherness."

"Yes, I know," John said, "but how do you know that you have the right way to worship? After all, look at how many religions there are and they all have different ideas of how to worship. How do you know your way is not wrong and Buddhism, or perhaps Judaism, is right? Maybe if you're not a Buddhist, you will go to hell when you die."

"I'm not worried about it," Margie answered.

"But if you love nature, and you love people, isn't that enough?" John asked.

"The trouble with that," Margie answered, "is that you don't have any ideal standards to focus on to try to live your life by."

"I can't buy that," said John. "Just look at the perfection of nature and it sets the standard. You don't need any scripture. Scriptures are written by people, and people can be wrong. Besides, scriptures can be interpreted any way people want, to serve their own purposes."

"Not the people who wrote the Bible," said Margie. "They had Divine guidance from God through his son Jesus."

"That reminds me of a funny story," John said. "In my hometown of Montague, there was an old sea captain who in his younger days had run cargo ships across Lake Michigan. One time he told my dad about getting into a terrible storm. And believe me," John said, "Lake Michigan can get mighty rough at times. It got so bad, the captain thought they might founder, so he ordered all the passengers to assemble on the fan tail, and had them put on life preservers. He yelled out above the storm, 'Is there a clergyman among you? If there is, I want you to pray.'

"An elderly man shouted back, 'I'm not a preacher, but I sure know how to pray. I'm a Baptist.'

"'Then do it,' the captain bellowed.

"The Baptist looked upward and shouted against the storm, 'God, we need your help. Please help us, but, God, don't send your son Jesus because this ain't no kid's job.'"

Margie tittered.

The sun had set and twinkling lights were coming on all over the city. Out toward the Golden Gate, Alcatraz Island looked lonely and desolate. Across the bay to the north, the lights of Sausalito twinkled, and off in the distance, the mauve-colored mass of Mount Tamalpais was barely visible in the twilight. To the right the city of Oakland produced a glow in the sky. John put his arm around Margie's waist and they felt a commingling of happiness.

For a long time, they sat in silence enjoying each other and enjoying the perfect night. Margie put her head on John's shoulder and time passed in a reverie.

At last, Margie said, "I think we should be getting back."

As they drove down from Twin Peaks, John knew that during that lovely night something had happened to him that separated all of life before this moment, by a gossamer membrane, from all that would follow. He left Margie at her door and they kissed good night.

A week went by before John saw Margie again. By now confident in his approach, he asked if she would like to spend a Saturday bike riding in Golden Gate Park—was she up to it after her stay in the hospital? Margie assured him that she felt fine.

They drove out to the park on a foggy but bracing day, rented bicycles, and set out to explore the lakes and paths. Margie was obviously happy, but not as energetic as John, who from time to time rode circles around her with cavorting energy. They stopped at the Japanese Tea Garden for a refreshing cup and a cookie, and they played on the arched footbridge. They sat for a while at Seal Rocks and watched the sleek animals rolling and playing in the ocean waves.

When they started back, John said, "Margie, I would like to buy you a gift. What would you like?"

She looked pleased but was quiet and unresponsive for a moment. Then she said, "Do you know what I would like?"

John admitted that he did not.

"I would like a teddy bear," she told him.

"It's yours," John said, and he gently pushed her into the Cliff House gift shop.

From an assortment of the creatures, she carefully selected a little fuzzy white specimen with black button eyes and nose. The saleslady placed it in a paper sack and handed it to her, but when she stepped outside, she immediately discarded the sack and clutched it to her as if it were a baby.

Margie held the animal figure to her and guided the bike with her other hand.

John asked if he could carry it for her.

"No," she answered firmly. "I want to carry him."

A strange quiet ensued, and John began to feel the chill of the fog. Even at her apartment door, she clung to the teddy bear with an uncommon attendance. She thanked John for the nice outing and the gift, but she looked troubled and was quiet, and yet she gave him a good-bye kiss and a warm hug.

Another week passed and he did not see her. John began to wonder if she was avoiding him for some reason. He worried that he had done something to offend her. But in the evening of the following Friday, there was a knock on his door and, upon opening it, there was Margie. John was delighted and asked her in.

"No," she said, "but would you do something for me?"

"Of course," he answered.

"Will you drive me to the Greyhound bus station in the morning?"

"Sure," he said, "but where are you going?"

He was astonished when she answered, "To Chicago. I'm going back to find my father."

"What happened?" John asked.

She ignored his inquiry. "Just take me to the bus station in the morning. I'll tell you about it then."

She left him standing in his doorway, feeling bewildered.

In the morning, after a restless night, John put her few belongings in his truck; they consisted of a small battered suitcase, a purse, and the teddy bear, which she now had covered with an infant's blanket, and carried as if it were animate.

As she was buying her ticket to Chicago, John's mind

drifted with the fog: Bus stations and train stations are islands of dismal beginnings and happy endings—families and couples pulled apart before a trip, and families and couples reunited after a trip; human emotions pulled from each other and joined again like the wisps of San Francisco fog, always swirling to what end? Was there meaning in the endless travels of people, or was it all just a mindless chaotic stirring of energy?

"Why?" John asked when she returned to him with her ticket.

"A number of reasons," she answered. "First, I can't let myself get drawn into another disaster."

"You mean, the motorcycle guy?" John asked. "I never could understand what you liked about him."

"No—no," Margie responded. "What you really don't understand is women and their instinct to nurture and influence males toward becoming and making families. I looked at Chuck's bad behavior the same way that I would look at an intractable child. Because children are bad, you don't just discard them. You work with them to develop their best qualities. Women are future-oriented, toward creating a family. My relation with Chuck was to draw him toward domesticity and family life.

"Men tend to be more centered on things. They are concerned with using whatever resources that exist around them to make the practical tools for immediate survival. I remember reading a story on tribal history in which men even drew pictures on cave walls of the various forms of animal manure, to catalogue it, to help them in hunting."

"I see," said John, "but I have never thought of my role, as a male, to be one of following a trail of spoor manure to shoot a bear."

Margie giggled. "You know what I mean," she said stamping her foot. "Males are always concerned with what is. Women are concerned with what can be—with making a family. I knew Chuck was mean, but I thought I could change him, and I still think that, even though he used to slap and punch me when he was drunk; I always had faith that if I was just good to him he would respond and change."

John spoke forlornly. "I don't have that much faith in humanity. My stepmother was mean from the first day I knew her to the day she died. Remember when we talked while we were up on Twin Peaks, and I asked if you thought God created poor crippled and diseased children? I try not to be bitter about it, but He also seems to have created some men, like the motorcycle guy, who are just natural sons of bitches."

"Yes," said Margie, "but do you remember, also, that I replied that of course we live in a world that has both good and bad in it, so you need a Divine religious standard for guidance to live by, and that is what gives me faith that people like Chuck can change."

"But what about us?" John asked. "I thought we were doing so well together."

"Look, I'm not right for you and you must know it, and besides, you have been back in the hills so long that you need to get out in the world and experience living before you become attached to me or anyone else. All that I would do in your life is narrow your social life to just me. That would be another disaster, and it too would be my fault. Besides, our religious views would forever be incompatible. Just wait," Margie said, "sooner or later you will meet the girl who is just right for you. When it happens you will both be certain about it."

Margie picked up her suitcase, hugged the teddy bear to her, and gave John a kiss. She stepped into the bus, the driver swung the door closed, and drove out of the station, leaving John standing there, forlorn and bewildered.

Lonely and frustrated, he waited in the coming months for a letter, a postcard, anything by which he could get in touch with her, but none ever came. The months passed with ever more depressing war news: the fall of France and the horror of the air battle over Britain. Then on the 7th of December 1941, John listened to the slow somber tone of President Roosevelt speaking of "A day that will live in infamy," after the Japanese naval attack on Pearl Harbor.

San Francisco had seemed so far from Europe and from the war, but suddenly everyone became aware of their vulnerable proximity to a war in the Pacific. Air-raid alarms were hurriedly set up and block wardens appointed. Army troops began moving ominously through the city.

In a flurry of silly responses, people began taping pieces of blue cellophane over the headlights of their cars, supposedly to prevent Japanese pilots from seeing their auto lights.

John quickly decided he should volunteer for military service. He went to a navy recruiting office where he heard about a new branch of the navy called the Construction Battalion, or Sea Bees. Within a day he was signed up. Within a month he was en route to Rhode Island with a trainload of recruits on their way to boot camp. Back on the West Coast, after a vigorous military indoctrination, his battalion was shipped overseas to the Aleutian Islands. It was a great adventure with mostly middle-aged men who were already highly skilled in every field of construction. If their military sharpness was questionable, their construction knowledge and energy was superb.

John's penchant for writing drove the mail censors crazy. Their idea of a letter home was a brief single page saying in essence, "I'm fine and hope you are the same." John never stopped there. He described his circumstances in detail and so his letters arrived at his brother's house in California looking like slices of Swiss cheese with innumerable censure holes that had been scissored out of them.

After about a year of building airfields, roads, shipping docks, et cetera, his battalion was shipped home for reassignment and John visited his brother's family on a short leave. There he met a girl who was living with his brother's family and who had been reading all of his letters from overseas. He knew at once she was the one he wanted to marry.

Everything in wartime is speeded up. Within a week they were engaged. Within two months they were married.

The minister who married them was very skeptical of this flighty marriage of an eighteen-year-old village girl to a sailor of questionable character. Before he would conduct the marriage, he took them aside and delivered a severe lecture on the responsibilities of marriage and family. But within a year or so, the minister was divorced and some fifty years later, John and Barbara were still enjoying marriage and family. The years were a string of pearls.

Margie was right when she said, "Sooner or later you will meet the girl who is just right for you."

To each his own.